Now
VEGAN!

Now VEGAN!

FRESH AND HEALTHY

LYNDA STONER

NEW HOLLAND

First published in Australia in 2008 by
New Holland Publishers (Australia) Pty Ltd
Sydney • Auckland • London • Cape Town

1/66 Gibbes Street Chatswood NSW 2067 Australia
218 Lake Road Northcote Auckland New Zealand
86 Edgware Road London W2 2EA United Kingdom
80 McKenzie Street Cape Town 8001 South Africa

National Library of Australia Cataloguing-in-Publication entry

Stoner, Lynda.
Now vegan! fresh and healthy / Lynda Stoner.

ISBN: 9781741106497 (hbk.)

Includes index.

Vegan cookery.

641.5636

Publisher: Fiona Schultz and Linda Williams
Publishing Manager: Lliane Clarke
Editor: Kay Proos
Designer: Natasha Hayles
Photographs: Graeme Gillies
Food Stylist: Amanda Biffin
Food Assistant: Annalisa McMillan
Production Assistant: Liz Malcolm
Printer: Power Printing Co., China

10 9 8 7 6 5 4 3 2

Our thanks to: Accoutrement Mosman, Wheel & Barrow Chatswood, Villaroy & Boch Chatswood, Mud
Australia and Tolle n Crowe Northbridge for the provision of fine crockery and materials for this book.

To my beloved son Luke, my parents Vang and Reg, Lesley, Dottie, Susie, Kate, Joey, Peter and our whole amazing extended family. Food has so often been the centrepiece around which we've nurtured, shared wisdom, laughed, exchanged points of view and just chilled out together.

My deepest thanks to my wonderful friends and fellow vegans/animal rights activists for your generosity and enthusiasm in sharing your scrumptious recipes.

To Linda Williams without whom this book simply would not have happened.

To Fiona Schultz, Lliane Clarke and the New Holland team for *Now Vegan!*'s elegant production.

To Animal Liberation.

And to the billions and billions of animals that suffer hourly so humans can continue to consume and wear animal products.

Contents

Introduction

Two questions vegans most often are asked are—
what do you eat? And why are you vegan?
The answer to the first is answered more
efficiently by asking—what don't vegans eat?
The only things we don't eat are animal products.

Most vegans I know are foodie hedonists and light years away from the fading fallacy of pale, anaemic and frail. They are among the fittest and healthiest people on the planet and they enjoy their food with extra relish knowing they are not contributing to environmental devastation, savage cruelty to animals and damage to their own health.

I have included in this book wisdom from throughout the ages from some of the greatest thinkers of all time, all of whom urge people to make the simple change to vegetarianism/veganism. It was difficult to choose a single quote but Einstein said, 'nothing will benefit human health and increase human chances for survival for life on earth as much as the evolution to a vegetarian diet.' Had he been alive today he would surely have said 'a vegan diet'.

Every time you have dairy products, or a piece of meat, you are directly contributing to the ever-increasing fragility of this planet. Meat production and dairy farming are major contributors to greenhouse emissions and massive users and polluters of water. It takes 4,000 glasses of water to produce 1 glass of milk. It takes 550 litres of water to produce enough flour or a loaf of bread and 7000 litres of water to produce 100 grams of beef. Last year the dairy industry spent more than $500 million on grains and concentrates and was the single biggest user of feed grain of all the animal industries. We are the only species on earth that continues to suckle once we have been weaned —and we do it from another species. What could be more unnatural?

Meat and dairy production are sucking the life out of animals, the planet and causing chronic illness to the peoples of those nations that consume the most animal protein. They are the countries that suffer the highest rates of cancer, diabetes 1 and 2, osteoporosis, asthma, coronary heart disease, kidney disease, constipation and high cholesterol among others.

Both the meat and dairy industries mutilate animals without anaesthesia and cause terrible suffering. Most people are aware of the Frankenstein cruelty of intensively producing chicken meat, pig meat and battery eggs yet there is still a misconception that dairy cattle have a 'normal' life. Nothing could be further from the truth. Cattle should live for around two decades but in contemporary dairy farms they are used up by eight years and what's left of them after slaughter is 'low quality meat'. Male calves are collateral and slaughtered at five days old or reared until three months of age for veal.

It is a travesty that animals must endure torture, suffering and ongoing exploitation so that prosperous societies can consume second hand protein that damages the environment, causes health problems and contributes to malnutrition in developing countries.

'The dairy cow is exposed to more abnormal physiological demands than any other class of farm animal', says John Webster, Emeritus Professor of Animal Husbandry, Bristol University's Clinical Veterinary Science Department.

I've been a vegetarian for over three decades and a vegan for five years. I recall the hysteria my dietary choices caused back then. People telling me I'd get rickets or anaemia or just expire from not woofing down bits of animals. And no, fish are not vegetables. They are sentient beings that suffer terribly either by having a hook thrust through their very tender mouths containing more nerve endings than we have, or through being netted—either way they suffocate.

The hysteria reached fever pitch though when I became pregnant. I was accused of being selfish and irresponsible, that I had no right to impose my beliefs on my unborn child and risk damaging him/her. Thankfully my husband shared my beliefs to live (and breed) without harming any other species. Our son Luke is a strapping, healthy and vibrant 23-year-old who, of his own volition, continues to not consume animal and fish flesh.

The need-to-consume meat and dairy propaganda comes from billion-dollar vested industries that are persuasive and pervasive. People often just accept without questioning the myths and fallacies. Back then it was the whole protein and iron deficiency thing. These days it's B12, zinc and omega-3. Meat and dairy industries are ramping up their marketing and they will continue to try to justify their exploitation of resources and cruelty to animals—you just have to be a bit more savvy.

Go vegan. It's easy. It's delicious. It's good for you, good for the planet and good for animals.

Here, in a nutshell, is where to get your nutritional needs (and yes, inside a nutshell is as good a place to start). I do not purport to be a qualified nutritionist but I am educated in fundamental healthy eating—there are many fine books and websites to access for more comprehensive information.

A good rule of thumb—soy protein, lots of fresh fruit and vegetables, whole grain foods, nuts and seeds daily—with all the diversity they provide—easy.

Where to Get Your Vitals

Protein

Human breast milk contains 5% protein; adult humans need only 2–3% protein, which you can get from a wide range of sources including: Nuts, legumes (lentils, red beans, chick peas, soy beans), wheat bulger, oats, seeds, pasta and the whole amazing array of soy protein prepackaged yummies from companies like AHIMSA (Asian supermarkets) and Sanitarium (check for no dairy in some of their products)—now literally hundreds of companies on the market cater for the ever growing vegan market.

And then there's tofu: the wonderful sweet/savoury things you can do with tofu are seemingly limitless. How lucky we are to have access to this abundance.

Calcium

One of the biggest furphies is that you need cow's milk to avoid osteoporosis—how is it then that 70 per cent of the world's population does not consume dairy and maintain low to nil incidence of osteoporosis? Excess animal protein (dairy and meat) makes the human body highly acidic which *actually leeches out calcium* from bones to alkalise the blood which in turn is passed out through urine.

Far safer to get your calcium from leafy green vegetables (in this and in so many ways broccoli is high on the 'Must Eat' list, as well as bok choy and spinach); bean curd (tofu); calcium enriched soy or rice milks; soy yoghurt; seeds; oranges; grains—wholegrain breads; dried figs.

While you're boning up your strength don't forget an hour's sun per day (done safely) is essential to getting Vitamins D and F.

Vitamin D

Forget that women shouldn't have muscles—that was last century. Physical strength in men AND women is just plain sexy—so lift your weights and move your butt and keep your bones strong.

Vitamin C

Most fruit contains Vitamin C. Bananas are packed with goodies including serotonin (the brain's feel-good chemical). Also found in leafy greens, potatoes and fresh salads.

Vitamin E

Go for nuts, vegetable oils, avocados, asparagus, whole grains and wheatgerm.

B Group

Yeast extract spread, whole grains, bell peppers, red and yellow peppers, legumes, leafy greens, mushrooms, fruit, nuts.

B12

Human bodies need only a minuscule amount of this vitamin (2–3 micrograms each day). Our bodies store small amounts in our livers, but without it your nervous system will suffer, and your chances of getting anaemia increased. B12 comes from bacteria (micro organisms). Go for yeast extract spread and other foods fortified with B12 including textured vegetable protein, soy milk, cereals and some vegan margarines.

Zinc

Whole grains, pumpkin and sunflower seeds, legumes, soybeans, tempeh and tofu, almonds, pecans, pistachios, walnuts, cashews, hazelnuts, macadamias, peanuts, corn, peas and sea vegetables.

Folate, Vitamin K, Minerals

Dark green vegetables, cereals, sea vegetables, quantities of soy protein and lots of fresh fruit and vegetables, nuts, seeds and whole grains.

Iron

Whole grains and cereals, wheatgerm, seeds, nuts, blackstrap molasses, chickpeas, raisons, prune juice, green leafy vegetables, tofu, miso, tomato juice.

Complex Carbohydrates and Fibre

Whole grain foods including breads, cereal, pasta, legumes, potatoes, rice, beans and peas. Fruit also contains high levels of fibre.

Omega 3 Fats

Fish is being flogged as 'brain food'—humane and healthy options include primrose oil, whole grain bread, pasta and rice, blueberries, tomatoes, avocadoes, bananas, broccoli, brussel sprouts, rockmelon and green vegetables, flaxseed oil and ground flaxseed, legumes, peas, potatoes, soy products, spinach, wheat germ rapeseed oil, walnuts, and tofu.

You can find many ingredients for these recipes from Western and Asian supermarkets, health food stores or go online to www.crueltyfreeshop.com.au and have vegan savouries, sweets, ready-made meals, personal and household products delivered to your door.

Soups

Chunky Mexican Bean Soup

Gluten free

Serves 6

Place the beans in a medium saucepan with 3 cups of water. Bring to the boil and cook, stirring occasionally and adding more water as needed, for approximately 40–50 minutes, or until tender (if the beans are previously soaked overnight they will cook a lot quicker).

Whilst the beans are cooking, in a large saucepan heat the olive oil and sauté the onions until lightly browned. Add the garlic and celery and sauté for a few minutes until fragrant. Now add the tinned tomatoes, water, lentils, capsicums, zucchini and carrot. Bring to the boil, then lower to a simmer. Stir regularly as the lentils tend to stick to the bottom. Cook for approximately 15 minutes or until the lentils are cooked.

Stir through the Mexican chilli powder and add salt to taste.

Garnish with heaps of coriander and serve with your favourite bread.

1½ cups of dried kidney beans, rinsed
2 tablespoons olive oil
1 brown onion, finely chopped
2 cloves garlic, minced
1 stick of celery, finely chopped (including the leaves)
2 x 400g (13oz) tins of diced tomatoes
2 cups of water
1 cup of dried red lentils, rinsed
1 red capsicum (bell pepper), diced
1 green capsicum, diced
1 zucchini (courgette), diced
1 carrot, finely sliced
Bunch of fresh coriander (cilantro), chopped (optional)
Mexican chilli powder (see note)

Note
I make my own Mexican chilli powder by combining the following:
¼ teaspoon pepper
2 teaspoons mild paprika powder
¼ teaspoon chilli powder
1 teaspoon cumin powder
1 teaspoon oregano powder

Quick and Yummy Soup

If you have unexpected guests and want to serve something substantial, this can be made quickly from ingredients you may have on hand in your fridge and cupboard.

Combine all the ingredients and heat through. Toast Turkish bread, spread with vegan cheese and melt under griller. Place one slice on top of each plate of soup, and garnish with some coriander leaves.

200g tin of coconut cream
400g tin savoury lentils
500g tin of vegetable soup
4 cups water
2 teaspoons vegetable salt
6 curry leaves
1 teaspoon chopped fresh chilli, optional
Leftover cooked vegetables such as carrots, potatoes,
  tomatoes, onions, and shallots
Turkish bread
Vegan cheese
Coriander (cilantro) leaves

Carrot and Cumin Soup

Heat oil in a large pan and cook the onion and garlic over a moderate heat until the onion is soft. Add the carrots, cumin and coriander and stir for 1 minute. Add stock, salt and pepper. Bring to the boil. Reduce heat and simmer gently for 30 minutes or until the carrots are soft. Blend the mixture in a food processor, add lemon juice, check seasoning.

Serve hot or chilled, garnished with chopped coriander and peanuts.

l tablespoon peanut oil

l large onion, chopped

l small clove garlic, minced

730g carrots, peeled and chopped (sweet potato can be used instead)

l tablespoon cumin seeds, toasted and ground

l tablespoon coriander seeds, toasted and ground

3 cups of veggie stock

Salt and pepper, to taste

l tablespoon freshly squeezed lemon juice

¼ cup of coriander, chopped

¼ cup roasted peanuts, chopped

l was so moved by the intelligence, sense of fun and personalities of the animals l worked with on Babe that by the end of the film l was a vegetarian.

James Cromwell, actor

Russian Borscht

Pour the water into a large heavy pot. Crush the bay leaf, drop it in the water and bring to the boil. Lower the heat and stir in the beets, carrots, tomatoes and onions. Simmer for about 5 minutes or until the vegetables are tender. Stir in the cabbage, lemon juice, sugar and seasoning. Simmer for another 5 minutes or until the cabbage is tender. Be sure to remove the bay leaf before serving. May be served hot or chilled, with or without a dollop of vegan sour cream.

3 cups water

1 bay leaf

2 cups grated fresh beets

1 cup diced carrots

1 cup diced tomatoes

½ cup minced onions

2 cups shredded green cabbage

2 tablespoons fresh lemon juice

1 tablespoon sugar

Salt and pepper, to taste

Dollop of vegan sour cream, optional

A human can be healthy without killing animals for food.

Leo Tolstoy, novelist and philosopher

Savoury Lentil Soup

Peel the onions. Cut into small pieces and cook in the oil for approximately 10 minutes. Add the vegetable stock and well-washed lentils and cook over a slow heat until tender, adding the chopped sage towards the end of the cooking. Rub through a sieve or liquidise in a food processor and return to the pan or freeze at this stage if desired. Just before serving, add the yeast extract and seasoning to taste, together with extra vegetable stock if necessary.

2 onions
2 tablespoons corn oil
1.7 litres (3 pints) vegetable stock
225g (7oz) red lentils
Fresh or dried sage, chopped
1 teaspoon yeast extract
Salt and pepper, to taste

Corn and Split Pea Chowder

In a saucepan lightly fry curry powder in olive oil, add creamed corn, sweet corn and split peas— simmer for 5 minutes. Mix vegetable stock cubes with water and add milk. Simmer for 10 minutes.

Variations—add mashed potatoes—puree if preferred.

Season to taste with salt or pepper or a little coconut milk.

1 ½ teaspoon curry powder
1 tablespoon olive oil
1 cup creamed corn
½ cup sweet corn
2 cups cooked yellow split peas
1 ½ vegetable stock cubes
1 cup soy milk
½ cup water

Soups

Riz-U-Marsh

(Mung Bean and Brown Rice Soup)

Serves 6

Wash the mung beans and rice and soak separately overnight. Next day, wash the mung beans again, removing the loose skins and drain.

In a large pot, boil 8 cups of the water. Add the mung beans and bring to the boil again. Lower heat and cook for 1 hour.

Drain the rice and add to the pot with the other 2 cups of water and the salt. Bring to the boil again. Lower heat and simmer for 30–40 minutes, stirring occasionally. The result should be a thick soup.

In a small frying pan, heat the oil and fry the onion, garlic and pepper until light golden in colour. Add the cumin and mix well. Pour this into the soup. Cover the pot and simmer on low heat for 5 minutes. Serve hot.

1 cup mung beans
½ cup rice
10 cups water
1½ teaspoon salt
3 teaspoons olive oil
1 medium onion, chopped finely
1 clove garlic, crushed
¼ teaspoon ground pepper, to taste
1 teaspoon ground cumin

There is no doubt that reducing consumption of meat, especially red meat, is one of the most effective things the individual can do to reduce their greenhouse gas pollution. Professor Ian Lowe, President, Australian Conservation Foundation

Thai Pumpkin Soup

Serves 6

Place the water, pumpkin, potato, onion, and stock cube in a large pot and boil until the vegetables are soft. Remove the vegetables with a slotted spoon and puree in a food processor, adding lemongrass, coriander and ginger. Return to the boiling pot and mix in the coconut milk. Add salt and chilli last and garnish with a sprig of parsley.

2 litres (3½ pints) water
1kg (2lbs) pumpkin, peeled and cut into large chunks
1 medium potato
1 medium onion
1 vegetable stock cube
2 tablespoons chopped lemongrass
½ cup coriander, chopped
1 teaspoon ginger, chopped
½ cup coconut milk
Salt
Chilli powder, to taste

I don't eat meat, fish or eggs. I was never a big meat-eater, but I've got more energy now.

Shania Twain, married to long time vegetarian and music producer Mutt Lange

Italian Pumpkin and Bean Soup

Place the beans in a medium saucepan with 3 cups of water. Bring to the boil and cook, stirring occasionally adding more water as needed, for 40–50 minutes or until tender.

Lightly sauté the garlic in the oil. Add the pumpkin and stir to coat with the oil. Pour in stock and tomato puree, cover and cook until pumpkin is almost tender. Add the pasta and cook until al dente. Season with the salt, pepper and herbs, then stir in the spinach and kidney beans. If desired, garnish with cream cheese.

2–3 cloves of garlic, smashed
1½ tablespoons extra virgin olive oil
500g (1lb) pumpkin, peeled and chopped
750ml (25fl oz) vegetable stock (see note)
250ml (8fl oz) tomato puree
125g (4oz) small pasta (eg penne piccoline)
Salt and pepper, to taste
Oregano or basil, fresh or dried
1½ cups of dried kidney beans, rinsed
1 bunch of English spinach leaves, washed and torn into pieces
Vegan cream cheese (optional)

Note
Vegetable stock can be made with stock cubes or by bringing to the boil 1 litre (1¾ pints) of water with some chopped vegetables. This can be any of a selection such as onion, carrots, celery, leeks, and some fresh herbs. Reduce to a simmer and cook until vegetables are tender.

Parsnip Soup

Warm stock over low heat and add all other ingredients. Cook for 20 minutes.

For a chunky soup mash with a potato masher or for a smooth, dinner-party-style blend in blender.

Garnish with fresh coriander.

3½ cups vegetable stock
600g (1¼lbs) parsnips, peeled and chopped
1 cooking apple, quartered, cored and chopped
1 onion, chopped
1 clove garlic
300ml (10fl oz) soy milk
2 teaspoons ground coriander
1 teaspoon ground cumin
1 teaspoon ground turmeric
Pinch salt
Few grinds of black pepper
Coriander leaves

Entrées

Vietnamese Rice Paper Rolls

Makes 15

Cover rice vermicelli with boiling water and set aside for 10 minutes or until tender. Refresh under cold running water. Drain well and transfer to a bowl. Add lemon juice and toss to coat.

Mix all dipping sauce ingredients in small bowl.

Dip each rice paper wrapper, one at a time, in large bowl of hot water until soft. Remove and place between sheets of paper towels to dry.

To assemble, take 1 rice paper wrapper and place a little of the snow peas, cucumber, bean sprouts, capsicum, mint and basil down the centre and top with a little vermicelli. Roll up tightly to form neat roll.

Place on a tray and cover with damp tea-towel. Repeat this process with the remaining rice paper wrappers.

Serve with Dipping Sauce.

125g (4oz) rice vermicelli
Juice of 2 lemons
15 sheets rice paper, small (16cm/6ins) and square
125g (4oz) snow peas (mange tout)
1 Lebanese cucumber, halved and cut into match-sticks
½ red capsicum (bell pepper)
½ cup firmly packed mint leaves
½ cup Thai basil leaves
500g (8oz) bean sprouts

Dipping Sauce
2 tablespoons soy sauce
2 tablespoons apple cider vinegar
1 teaspoon fresh grated ginger
2 tablespoons warm water
2 teaspoons raw sugar

I haven't bought any leather articles for a very long time. My ideal is to be able to avoid all animal products, in food as well as clothing. Martina Navratilova

Entrées

Beetroot Tapenade

Roast the unpeeled beetroot on rock salt until soft—approximately 40 minutes in a moderate oven, 180°C (350°F) Gas Mark 4. Cool and peel, then cut into thin slices, and add the capers. Sweat the shallot in the oil and then add in the garlic. Combine with beetroot and lemon juice.

1 large beetroot
Rock salt
1 tablespoon capers, chopped
100ml (3fl oz) olive oil
1 shallot (spring onion), sliced
1 clove garlic, minced
Squeeze of lemon juice

Olive Tapenade

Blend all ingredients together in a food processor, adding the oil slowly to form a paste. This is great as a dip or spread. Keeps well in the fridge.

2 cups black or green pitted olives
1 cup capers, drained
1 small clove garlic
Freshly cracked pepper
1 cup olive oil, approximately

From left: Beetroot Tapenade, Coriander and Peanut Pesto (see recipe page 34), Olive Tapenade

Entrées

Coriander and Peanut Pesto

Makes 2 cups

Coat peanuts in shallow baking tin in oven preheated at 180°C (350°F) Gas Mark 4 for 15–20 minutes, leave to cool. Blend all other ingredients in a food processor. When paste is smooth, add peanuts and blend, adding oil slowly.

200ml (6fl oz) peanut oil
40g (1½oz) raw blanched peanuts
2 green chillies
2 cloves of garlic
1 tablespoon fresh ginger
100g (3oz) basil leaves
25g (1oz) mint leaves
1 tablespoon palm sugar
30ml (1fl oz) lime Juice
100g (3oz) coriander

Broad Bean Puree with Rocket

Serves 4

This is a classic Italian dish. Serve warm with crusty bread. Use fresh or frozen broad beans.

If possible, soak the beans overnight, then drain. Cook them in fresh water until tender, approximately 25 minutes. Drain and puree, then add salt and pepper.

Place rocket in a pot with 2 tablespoons of the olive oil. Cook until tender.

Spoon the puree onto plates, top with greens and drizzle with remaining olive oil.

2 cups broad beans
Salt and pepper, to taste
¼ cup olive oil
500g (1lb) rocket (you can also use cress or chicory)

Entrées

Aubergine Paté

Cook the eggplant in oil, remove the skin and puree the flesh. Peel and chop the onion and cook it in oil until soft and transparent. Add the eggplant puree and the tomato paste and cook gently for a few minutes to let the flavours mingle. Season with salt, pepper, coriander and parsley. A delicious topping for wholemeal bread.

I eggplant (aubergine), sliced
I onion
A little olive oil or walnut oil
I teaspoon tomato paste
Sea salt
White pepper
Ground coriander, to taste
I dessertspoon chopped flat-leaved parsley

I have been a vegetarian for about ten years. I lost weight really fast. My mother died from cancer so this is all very personal to me. And I would just like the planet to be a better place. Linda Blair

Nasudengaku (Eggplant grilled with Special Miso Paste)

Serves 2

Put miso, sugar, sake and mirin in saucepan and mix them together on simmer to medium heat. Be careful not to burn them. Take saucepan off the stove when it starts to boil.

Cut the eggplant in half and cut into the flesh in a chess board pattern in order for heat to penetrate. Deep fry the eggplant in oil for 20 seconds. Put them into microwave oven for 1–1½ minutes so that the inside of the eggplant cooks through.

Pour the special paste on top of both slices of eggplant with garnish on top.

Serve with a spoon.

100g miso (available from Asian supermarkets)
25g (1oz) sugar
30ml (1fl oz) sake
30ml (1fl oz) mirin
1 eggplant (aubergine), cut in half
Vegetable oil
Green garnish for decoration

Nothing will benefit human health and increase chances for survival of life on Earth as much as the evolution to a vegetarian diet. Albert Einstein

Guacamole Dip (Gluten free)

In a bowl, place the avocados and mash with a fork or potato masher until smooth. Add the lemon juice, salt and pepper. Toss through the shallots, tomato, capsicum and some of the parsley.

Serve in a small bowl, garnish with a few sprigs of parsley, and eat with lightly salted corn chips or sticks of crisp vegetables such as carrot and celery.

2 avocados, peeled and seeded
Juice from half a lemon
Salt and pepper, to taste
2 shallot stalks, chopped finely
1 tomato, diced
½ red capsicum, diced
1 small bunch of continental parsley, chopped finely (reserve some for garnish)

Pesto

Blend basil and garlic in food processor. Add pine nuts and olive oil halfway through, with cheese if using. If it won't blend thoroughly add more olive oil.

40 basil leaves
4 cloves garlic
1 cup pine nuts
2 tablespoons olive oil
Vegan cheese in small doses, or just sprinkle vegan parmesan on the finished product (optional)

Caramelised Onion Bruschetta

Using a heavy-based saucepan, fry the onions on a low heat until they are golden and caramelised. Be careful not to burn them. This will take approximately 25 minutes.

Slice French loaf into segments and spoon the bruschetta mix between the segments, wrap in tin foil and put in oven on low heat. Grill the garlic bread and top with onions.

4 brown onions, thinly sliced
1 tablespoon olive oil
Garlic oil
1 vegan French loaf

Char-Grilled Capsicum with Sunflower Dip

Makes 1 cup

Char-grill the capsicum whole over a flame or under a hot grill until skins are black. Put in a plastic bag or sealed container for 10 minutes while still hot to sweat them. This way the skins will peel off easily. Remove skins and seeds.

Roughly chop the capsicums and put in a blender with lemon juice, garlic and sunflower seeds. Blend. Stir, then blend again adding olive oil slowly to form a smooth consistency. Season and stir through the fresh basil.

3–4 capsicums (bell peppers)
Juice of 1 lemon
½ clove garlic
¾ cup sunflower seeds, toasted
½ cup olive oil
Salt and pepper, to taste
½ cup basil, roughly chopped

I've been vegan for about ten and a half years. It's been all good. I'm obviously much healthier.

Woody Harrelson

Baba Ghanoush

Serves 4

Rub the eggplant with the olive oil and bake on a tray in a medium hot oven, 200°C (400°F) Gas Mark 5 until the centre is tender, about 30–40 minutes. Chop roughly using the skins too. Blend thoroughly with all the garlic, lemon and tahini. Smooth onto a plate, dribble a few drops of olive oil on top and sprinkle with a little paprika. Serve with wholemeal pita bread and tabouli.

A few drops of olive oil
1 large eggplant (aubergine)
1 small clove of garlic, crushed
Juice of 1 lemon
1 tablespoon dark tahini
Pinch of salt and pepper
Pinch of paprika and a little olive oil, to garnish

My wife actually got worried about my drinking so much regular milk, you know, so she got me into rice milk and now soy milk, which I greatly enjoy. A soy mocha's a fine thing. Willie Nelson

Side Dishes

Rosemary and Garlic Potatoes

Serves 6

Bring a pan of salted water to the boil. Cut potatoes into large chunks and boil in salted water with the garlic for 10 minutes. Drain potatoes well and place in a roasting pan with a generous amount of oil. Add salt to taste, rosemary and toss. Roast for 35–40 minutes or until golden and crunchy.

2kg (4lbs) Desiree, Nicola or Spunta potatoes, peeled
2 heads garlic, broken into cloves and peeled
Olive oil
Salt, to taste
5 sprigs rosemary

I take vitamins daily, but just the bare essentials not what you'd call supplements. I try to stick to a vegan diet heavy on fruit, vegetables, tofu and other soy products. Clint Eastwood

Mushrooms

2 tablespoons vegan margarine
1kg (2lbs) sliced mushrooms
2 tablespoons soy sauce
½ bunch parsley, chopped
Juice of 1 lemon
Black pepper, to taste

A quick and scrumptious side dish that is literally mouthwatering...

In a non-stick frying pan, put tiny amount of margarine, barely enough to cover surface, and add mushrooms. Sprinkle with soy sauce, chopped parsley, lemon juice and black pepper. Cook until mushrooms are browned and serve hot.

Asparagus

Some cooks break the ends off asparagus, others cut the ends; as long as the hard bits are removed do whatever feels best for you. Place asparagus in a shallow, ovenproof dish, add salt and pepper and dot with vegan margarine. Cover with foil and cook in preheated oven at 150°C (300°F) Gas Mark 2 for 20 minutes.

Every time we sit down to eat, we make a choice. Please choose vegetarianism. Do it for animals. Do it for the environment and do it for your health.

Alec Baldwin

Corn

¼ cup vegan margarine
2 onions, chopped
I small pack corn kernels
I heaped tablespoon soy bacon bits
I level dessertspoon yeast extract
Pepper, to taste

Melt vegan margarine and add onions, stirring until they are soft and translucent. Add corn, soy bacon bits and yeast extract. Stir until corn is coated. You may wish to add pepper but not salt because the yeast extract should make it sufficiently salty. Serve hot.

Celery

½ cup vegetable oil
5 sticks celery, washed, ends removed and cut into 5cm (2in) pieces
I large onion, roughly chopped
2 tablespoons wholemeal flour
300ml (10fl oz) vegetable stock
½ teaspoon yeast extract

Heat oil and fry celery until almost soft (be careful as it 'spits'). Add onion and cook until soft and translucent. Add flour and stir until absorbed. Gradually add stock and stir until thickened. Stir in yeast extract. Serve hot.

As custodians of the planet, it is our responsibility to deal with all species with kindness.

Richard Gere

Mema Lorrie's Tsimmis

Place a layer of yams on the bottom of a large Dutch oven. Then place a layer of carrots, then a layer of pineapple with the juice. Next add a generous layer of brown sugar. Place pats of vegan margarine on top of brown sugar layer. Then repeat all layers again—yams, carrots, pineapple, brown sugar and margarine. Repeat again.

Bring to low boil, lower heat and simmer, partially covered. Every once in a while grab the handles of pot and 'shake' or 'shimmy' the pot and its contents. DO NOT MIX. Every once in a while mixture will start to dry out, so add some orange juice to keep it moist.

Mema Lorrie says to 'cook it until it dies.' However, the longer and slower it cooks, the better. Basically, it should cook for at least 2–3 hours to meld all the flavours together.

Feeds a lot of people or just a few hungry ones. Enjoy!

1½ kg (3lbs) yams or sweet potatoes, peeled and cut into thick slices or chunks
1 kg (2lbs) canned pineapple chunks, sweetened or unsweetened (retain juice)
2 large cans carrots—slice and discard water (or 1kg or 6 to 8 large carrots, peeled and sliced)
¾ firmly packed cup brown sugar
1–2 cups—(as required) orange juice
120g vegan margarine

Potatoes with Capers

Boil potatoes with herbs until soft. Cook onions in oil until translucent. Drain potatoes and cut into quarters and return to pot where you have melted vegan margarine. Add onions, shallots, capers, pepper and salt and roll potatoes around until covered. Serve hot.

1½kg (3lbs) potatoes, peeled
1 teaspoon thyme
1 teaspoon dried basil
1 tablespoon vegan margarine
2 onions, chopped
1 tablespoon oil
2 stalks shallots, chopped finely
2 tablespoons capers
Salt and pepper, to taste

I am in favour of animal rights as well as human rights. That is the way of a whole human being.

Abraham Lincoln

Carrots

1kg (2lbs) carrots, peeled and cut into rings
125g (4oz) vegan margarine
Juice of 2 oranges
Rind of 1 orange, grated
1 tablespoon brown sugar

Boil carrots until almost soft, then drain. Melt vegan margarine in a pot and add carrots. Pour over orange juice, rind and brown sugar. Cover and cook on low heat for 10 minutes. Serve hot.

Baby Spinach

The taste of baby spinach compared to grown-up spinach is almost incomparable—suffice to say that even spinach 'haters' will change their minds about this vegetable when they try baby spinach.

It cooks down to a tiny amount, so commence with large amount in saucepan with very small amount of water and vegan margarine. Keep stirring—it cooks quickly—don't overcook the delicious taste out of it. Add black pepper and a small amount of vegan margarine.

It is my view that the vegetarian manner of living by its purely physical effect of the human temperament would most beneficially influence the lot of mankind.

Albert Einstein

Mains

Huevos Rancheros (Salt free)

Serves 1

Cut away the white pith inside the capsicums and scrape out seeds. Dice. How many hot or mild chillies you use is up to you depending on your comfort level. Dice the onion. Cut the coriander into confetti with scissors.

Pour some olive oil into a non-stick frying pan and heat slowly. Add the diced onion and stir. Cook the onion just enough to take the 'rawness' out. DON'T fry it. The secret is that the vegetables must not taste raw but they must not taste cooked either. Set aside.

Heat a saucepan of water and simmer just below boiling. Add the chopped capsicums, peppers and whole tomatoes and blanch them. Drain and add to the onion. Cut the tomatoes in half after blanching so their juice isn't lost in the saucepan. Add the garlic and coriander and a splash more olive oil and stir as it cools. Keep in an air-tight container in the fridge and stir every time you use it.

To serve: Place the bread on a large plate. Spoon a line of salsa from one side to the other. Then a line of lettuce. Roll up like a napkin and eat it, making sure the salsa doesn't dribble out onto your lap. You can also use the salsa as a relish to spark up heaps of other dishes.

½ red capsicum (bell pepper)
½ yellow capsicum (bell pepper)
½ green capsicum (bell pepper)
1 onion
1 clove garlic, crushed or minced
Good quality olive oil
2 long red chilli peppers
1 small hot green chilli pepper
3-4 on-vine cherry tomatoes
5 stalks coriander (cilantro)
1 large lettuce leaf, shredded
1 wrap of wheat, rye or corn organic vegan bread

Variations

You can put a couple of tablespoons of red wine vinegar into the water when blanching the capsicums. You can add a teaspoon of salt to the water and a teaspoon of mustard seed in the final mix. You can add ½ stick of diced celery and blanch it quickly. I actually leave two whole super hot chillies, like jalapenos, in the finished bottle but don't dish them up. I also now plant cloves of garlic and whole onions in balcony pots and use their new, fresh, green shoots for taste and colour.

Mains

54

Easy Mushroom Pie (Gluten free)

In a large saucepan, brown the onion in the oil. Add cracked pepper and sauté for a few seconds only (be careful not to burn and try not to breath it in as it's very potent!). Toss in the mushrooms and sauté until softened. Lightly drizzle the mix with some tamari.

In a separate cup make a paste with the cornflour and a little water. Add to the mushroom mixture to thicken. Throw in the lentils and warm through. Taste to see if you need to add more tamari.

Line a lightly greased pie dish with shortcrust pastry. Blind bake by taking a circle of baking paper weighted down with pastry offcuts or rice etc. placed in the dish with shortcrust pastry, then remove paper and weights after 5 minutes—this cooks the bottom a little before the filling goes in.

Spoon the mushroom mixture into the pastry case. Top with the puff pastry, moistening the edges with a little water and pressing down to seal. Brush pastry with a little water and sprinkle sesame seeds over it. Prick surface with a fork and bake in a hot oven 220°C (450°F) Gas Mark 6 until brown.

You may prefer to use the mixture to make pasties instead. In that case, cut the pastry into squares, spoon mixture onto one side of each square, fold in half diagonally to form triangles, moisten the edges and press down. Prick surface with a fork and bake as above.

1 brown onion, finely chopped
Olive oil
Cracked pepper, to taste
500g (1lb) button mushrooms, half finely chopped, half roughly chopped
400g (13oz) tin of brown lentils, rinsed and strained
1 tablespoon cornflour or arrowroot powder
Tamari, to taste
1–2 sheets vegan shortcrust pastry
1 sheet vegan puff pastry
1 teaspoon sesame seeds

Note

All amounts are approximate as the mushrooms shrink and let out a lot of moisture when cooking and it also depends how salty your tamari is, so you need to just taste and see!

Serve with roasted veggies or a salad. Tastes great with a little tomato sauce (just like the Aussie meat pie, only cruelty free). Enjoy!

Ratatouille

Serves 6

Slice eggplant into large slices and then into cubes. Salt eggplant and place in a colander over a bowl for 30 minutes to remove bitter juices. Rinse and blot dry.

Heat 2 tablespoons of the oil in a large pot. Add onions, capsicum and garlic and cook over medium to low heat for 15 minutes. Remove from pot and set aside.

Wash pot and heat 2 more tablespoons of the oil. Sauté zucchini over medium heat for 2–3 minutes on each side or until just browned. Don't stir, allow zucchinis to sit in place. Remove from pot and set aside.

Heat 2 more tablespoons of oil in the pot, and add a single layer of eggplant. Cook over medium heat, just until the eggplant is softened and browned on both sides; about 4 minutes. Repeat for any remaining eggplant.

Return all veggies to the pot with the eggplant. Add beans and tomatoes and cook uncovered over medium-high heat for 15 minutes, stirring every so often to allow flavours to meld. Don't overcook the veggies.

Remove from heat, season and stir in basil.

2 x 500g (1lb) eggplants (aubergines)
$^1\!/_2$–$^3\!/_4$ cups extra virgin olive oil
2 onions, sliced thinly
1 red capsicum (bell pepper), sliced
3 cloves garlic, minced
3 medium zucchini (courgette), halved lengthwise
    and cut into 2.5cm (1in) pieces
420g can of red kidney beans
500g (1lb) tomatoes, seeds removed and diced
Salt and pepper, to taste
$^1\!/_2$ cup chopped basil

Stuffed Zucchini

Serves 4

Boil zucchini for 5 minutes, drain and carefully cut into halves. Use knife to 'ring' edges, and cut flesh into squares (as you would mango) and carefully remove with a scoop or spoon while keeping base intact. Place bases into greased ovenproof casserole or baking dish. I find it helps keep it all together if you make individual 'boats' around them with aluminium foil.
Drain tomatoes and chop.

Heat margarine and fry the garlic, tomatoes and button mushrooms until soft. Mix with half of the breadcrumbs, zucchini flesh, lemon juice and parsley. Put into zucchini bases. Sprinkle over with remaining breadcrumbs, vegan parmesan and cover with slices of cheese. Cook in moderate oven, 180°C (350°F) Gas Mark 4 for 15 minutes.

Serve hot with salad.

4 large zucchini (courgette), retain ends
400g can tomatoes drained
1 tablespoon vegan margarine
2 cloves garlic, peeled and chopped
150g can chopped button mushrooms
4 tablespoons fine breadcrumbs
2 tablespoons fresh lemon juice
2 tablespoons finely chopped parsley
1 tablespoon Parmazano (vegan parmesan cheese)
Vegan Edam cheese

I'm a big health food freak and a vegetarian devotee.
Chelsea Clinton

Seitan in Red Wine with Rosemary

Serves 4

Boil potatoes for the mash. While they are cooking you can start the rest.

Place the seitan in a large baking dish. Mix together the stock, red wine, rosemary and garlic and pour over. Add the carrots, zucchini and beans and bake for about 30–40 minutes in a moderate oven, 180°C (350°F) Gas Mark 4 until the veggies are tender. Remove from oven and set aside.

Once the potatoes are cooked, mash them with vegan margarine, soy milk, salt and pepper.

To make the sauce, remove two cups of liquid from the baking dish, pour into a frying pan and bring to the boil. Mix cornflour with a little cold water until it forms a smooth paste and add to boiling liquid. Cook, stirring, until it thickens a little. Remove from heat and add mustard.

Place the mash on a plate and place the seitan and veggies on top then pour over some of the sauce. Serve this with a glass or two of the leftover organic red wine. Great for a winter's night in!

At least 2 potatoes per person
500g packet seitan (wheat meat)
1 teaspoon American mustard
1 bunch baby carrots, peeled
2 zucchinis (courgettes), sliced
Green beans, trimmed
2 cups veggie stock
1 cup organic red wine
3 teaspoons dried rosemary
2 teaspoons garlic, crushed
2 tablespoons cornflour

Potato Mash
Vegan margarine
Soy milk
Salt and pepper, to taste

Quick and Easy Vol Au Vents

Serves 6

Place mushrooms in saucepan with a little water and margarine and boil for 30 seconds. Let stand.

Slice tofu very finely and then into slivers. Fold the asparagus, tofu and mushrooms together. Add salt, pepper, cream cheese and soy milk and fold together. Let stand for at least half an hour.

Spoon mixture into cases, place in preheated oven at 200°C (400°F) Gas Mark 5 and cook for 10 minutes. This is nice served with hot baby boiled potatoes.

500g (1lb) mushrooms, finely sliced
1 tablespoon water
1 tablespoon vegan margarine
150g (5oz) smoked tofu
2 x 340g tins drained asparagus
Salt and cracked pepper, to taste
1 tablespoon soy cream cheese
2 tablespoons soy milk
6 vol au vent cases

Animals have the same source as we have. Like us, they derive the life of thought, will and love from the Creator. St. Francis Assisi

Mushroom Risotto

Throughout this process, ensure you grab yourself a glass of wine and make sure your guests join you in the kitchen. No fun slaving away by yourself!

Serves 4

Heat the oil and margarine in a saucepan. Add garlic and onion and fry briefly. Add rice, be sure to stir constantly whilst the rice is cooking so it absorbs the flavour of the onion, garlic and oil and becomes smooth and creamy and turns translucent. Slop by slop add all the veggie stock and then the silken tofu, continuing to stir the risotto the whole time. If needed, add more water. The above process should take approximately 20 minutes.

Put just enough water and soy sauce in a fry pan to cover of the base of the pan, heat. Add mushrooms and cook until flavour of soy sauce has been absorbed. Toast pine nuts under grill until light brown in colour.

To serve, scoop a serve of risotto rice onto each plate, shake over some vegan parmesan cheese and spread the mushrooms on top. Sprinkle over the pine nuts, coriander and shallots. Add salt and pepper.

Top up the wine and enjoy!

Another good addition is mashed avocado with a bit of lime juice and Tabasco sauce.

Risotto

1 generous splash extra virgin olive oil
2 dessertspoons vegan margarine
8 cloves garlic, finely chopped
1 red onion, finely chopped
2 cups risotto rice
6 veggie stock cubes (1 cube to ½ cup hot water)
300g packet silken tofu

Mushroom Topping

1 splash soy sauce
4 cups Swiss brown mushrooms, sliced
2 cups oyster mushrooms, sliced
1 cup pine nuts
4 tablespoons vegan parmesan cheese
1 cup of fresh coriander (cilantro), finely chopped
1 bunch of shallots, chopped
Salt and cracked pepper, to taste

Lentil Bobotie

Diana is proprietor of the famous Squirrels restaurants in South Brisbane and Newmarket, Queensland and Sydney and Wollongong, NSW. She is the author of six cookbooks. 'Bobotie' is one of the best known South African dishes, and like sosaties, chutneys, sambals and some preserves, it was brought there by Muslim slaves in the late 17th century. Traditionally made from leftover meat from the Sunday meal, this Bobotie has been adapted for vegans.

Serves 6–8

Cover lentils with water and cook for 30 minutes. Cut bread into squares and soak in soy milk in a baking dish. Finely dice the onions and garlic and cook in a frying pan in a little olive oil. Add the turmeric and cook for a minute. Drain the lentils and add to soaked bread. Add the remaining ingredients and mix in baking dish and flatten. Mix the topping ingredients and spread over the surface. Bake for an hour at 150°C (300°F) Gas Mark 2.

Base

2 cups brown or green lentils
3 slices wholemeal bread
I cup of soy milk
2 brown onions
6 cloves garlic
I tablespoon olive oil
I teaspoon turmeric powder
400g tin tomatoes
3 tablespoons vinegar
2 tablespoons chutney
2 tablespoons mild curry paste
2 tablespoons sultanas
Pepper and salt to taste

Topping

I teaspoon nutritional yeast
2 tablespoons tahini
2 tablespoons Dijon mustard
2 tablespoons soy sauce

Greek Stuffed Eggplant

Cut the eggplant in half lengthways, scoop out the flesh and dice. Reserve. Bake the eggplant skins in hot oven 200°C (400°F) Gas Mark 5 for about 30 minutes until soft. Cover the soy protein with warm water. Sauté the onions in oil, add the eggplant flesh and cook until soft. Add paprika and cook for a further 5 minutes. Add basil, drained lentils and soy protein and tomato paste. Sprinkle with pepper and salt. Top with cheese and bake until cheese melts.

2 eggplants (aubergines)
½ cup soy protein
2 onions, finely diced
½ cup olive oil
1 teaspoon sweet paprika
½ cup basil, chopped
1 cup cooked green lentils
140g tomato paste
Salt and pepper, to taste
4 slices dairy-free cheese

Red Lentil Dahl

Serves 6

Fry the onion in the oil until golden brown. Add the garlic, spices and seasoning and cook for 1 minute. Remove from heat.

Spread the red lentils out on a tray and carefully pick out any stones or twigs. Wash thoroughly and add to the onion mix. Mix through the tomato paste. Add enough water to cover the lentils and bring to the boil. Skim the scum, cover and gently simmer until the lentils are tender (about 30–40 minutes), adding enough water to keep the lentils moist and a bit 'saucy'. Serve hot with kofta or on its own with pappadams or corn chips.

1 tablespoon vegetable oil
1 medium onion, finely chopped
2 cloves garlic (crushed)
½ teaspoon ground turmeric
1 teaspoon ground paprika
1 teaspoon ground coriander
½ teaspoon ground cumin
2 bay leaves
Pinch black pepper
¼ teaspoon chilli flakes (optional)
½ teaspoon sea salt
1 cup red lentils
1–2 tablespoon tomato paste
Water as required

Tofu Kofta Bake

While in Melbourne I used to eat at the Friends of the Earth cafè in Smith Street. They kindly gave me my favourite fabulous recipe to pass on to other vegans.

Heat oil and sauté onion. Mash all ingredients together and press into oiled baking dish. Sprinkle with ground nuts and seeds. Bake for 30 minutes at 180°C (350°F) Gas Mark 4 or until browned.

Serve with the best organic tomato sauce you can find or a chutney of your choice. My favourite is Pineapple and Cumin chutney for zing power!

For a spicier version of this dish add: 4 tablespoons ground cumin, 1 tablespoon ground fennel seeds, 1 tablespoon cinnamon and 1 tablespoon turmeric. Cook the spices with the onion for 1–2 minutes before adding to the main mix.

1 tablespoon oil
1 onion, finely chopped
2 cups cooked mashed pumpkin
2 blocks firm tofu, crushed
1–2 cups of cooked rice, lentils or chickpeas
2 tablespoons white or buckwheat flour
½ cup toasted nuts and/or seeds (suggest linseeds, almonds and sunflower seeds), chopped
1 tablespoon miso
2 tablespoons tamari
Salt and pepper, to taste
Optional: cooked potato pieces, fried mushrooms or leftover veggie stew

Never Fail Vegan Pizza

This recipe was adapted from Vicki the Veggo's now out-of-print book Super Soy Foods. *This is my signature dish. I take it to every Vegan Society NSW meeting, our stalls and fundraisers. The secret of its success is kneading fresh herbs into the crust, so no part of the pizza is boring. It works!*

Preheat oven to moderately hot, 200°C (400°F) Gas Mark 5.

Mix the flour and oregano, then add vegan margarine, oil and milk or water. Mix in fresh herbs to form a soft dough, then knead for a few seconds. Roll out to about ½cm (¼in) thickness. Brush a pizza tray with olive oil, place the crust on and trim the edges. Put in the oven for a quick blast for say 5–6 minutes.

Remove from the oven and cover the crust with hummus. This ensures your crust will never be brittle and will remain moist as the hummus sinks through the dough while cooking. Add sauce and toppings then sprinkle sesame seeds on top. Season with salt and herb blend. Bake for 10 minutes.

Crust

1 ½ cups wholemeal self-raising flour
Pinch of dried oregano
2 tablespoon vegan margarine, melted
2 tablespoons oil
About ½ cup of soy milk or water
Herbs for the dough (coriander, basil, dill or oregano)
100g tub hummus
Sesame seeds for topping
Salt and herb blend for seasoning

Continued on page 70

A great pizza is not, as commonly thought, based on a cheese-based recipe. It's in making a homemade Italian style tomato sauce.

Heat oil in a frying pan and cook the onion, capsicum and garlic for 1 minute. Stir in tomatoes and basil and continue to cook for 2 minutes. Add the water and cook for 5 minutes, stirring. Continue to cook until a thick sauce is obtained.

Sauce

½ onion, chopped
½ capsicum (bell pepper), chopped
1 clove garlic, crushed
2–3 sun-dried or ripe tomatoes
Pinch of sweet dried basil
¼ cup water

Toppings

Here are my favourite toppings

Chopped tempeh or tofu
Mushrooms
Sliced olives or vegan olive paste
Chopped pineapple

Gourmet Vegan Quiche

Melt the vegan margarine and cream cheese together and add the flour. Shape mix into a ball and then take a handful of the mixture and place it on a flat surface. Sprinkle a little flour around so that the mixture does not stick and flatten with a rolling pin. Grease a 26cm x 26cm (10in x 10in) quiche tin and press in the pastry. Bake at 180°C (350°F) Gas Mark 4 for 20 minutes for the base then remove.

Pastry

2–3 cups of plain flour
250g vegan margarine
375g tub vegan cream cheese

Fry onion until translucent then add mushrooms. Add the garlic and the packet of 'tuna', then add the dill and the soy milk. If you find that the mixture is not thickening, you can make a paste of plain flour and oil and stir it through. Once brought to the boil you should find that it thickens the mixture perfectly.

Place this mix onto your base and put back in the oven for about 15–20 minutes.

Filling

1 packet of mock 'tuna', crumbled or sliced—
  or you can use veggie garlic loaf, diced
1 small red onion, diced
2 mushrooms, diced
Small amount of oil for frying
1 teaspoon garlic
1 cup soy milk
1–2 teaspoons dried dill

Creamed Vegetables with Gnocchi

Place the potatoes in a bowl and mash them. Stir in garlic, salt and pepper. Knead in the flour until dough-like consistency is reached.

Place deep saucepan, roughly filled halfway with water and a pinch of salt on stove and bring to the boil.

While waiting for it to boil you can now make the gnocchi balls. Wet hands slightly and roll 1 teaspoon of dough into a small, roughly bite-size ball. Repeat this with the rest of the mixture. Carefully place balls into the boiling water. Leave in for 3–4 minutes until they come to the surface. Scoop them out and gently coat with the cooking oil to prevent them from sticking together. Put aside.

Heat oil in frying pan or wok. Add all vegetable filling ingredients and cook for 5–7 minutes or until slightly cooked but still crisp.

Place all cream sauce ingredients into blender or food processor and mix until smooth. Stir the cream sauce through the vegetables. Pour over the gnocchi. Serve hot.

Vegetable Filling
2 tablespoons cooking oil
1 onion, chopped
7 medium sized mushrooms, chopped
2 garlic cloves, finely chopped
½ broccoli, cut into bite-sized florets
1 carrot, chopped
10 green beans, chopped
½ teaspoon vegetable stock
1 teaspoon coriander
Salt and pepper, to taste

Gnocchi
3 warm potatoes, diced and boiled
Salt and pepper, to taste
1 garlic clove finely diced, optional
1 saucepan of water
1 cup of potato flour or normal flour
1 teaspoon oil

Cream Sauce
2 warm potatoes, diced and boiled
1 cup soy milk
2 tablespoons vegan margarine
1 teaspoon vinegar or white wine, to taste
Salt and pepper, to taste

Spinach Stew

Heat oil in saucepan over medium heat. Add flour, stirring continuously until it has slightly browned. Next, add crushed garlic and stir until it has slightly browned too— 1–2 minutes. Add paprika and stir for 30 seconds, then put in one quarter of the spinach, again stirring continuously for 30 seconds. Pour half the water into the saucepan. Add rest of the spinach, stirring until a thick paste has formed. Add vegetable stock, soy sauce, coriander, caraway and salt. Cook for 4 minutes, stirring occasionally.

¼ cup oil
2 heaped tablespoons plain flour
3 cloves garlic, crushed
1 level teaspoon paprika
1 bunch of spinach, shredded
1 cup water
2 teaspoons vegetable stock
1 teaspoon soy sauce
1 teaspoon ground coriander
1 teaspoon ground caraway
Salt, to taste

Vegetarian food leaves a deep impression on our nature. If the whole world adopts vegetarianism, it can change the destiny of human kind. Albert Einstein

Vegetable Lasagne

Serves 3–4

Mix cornflour with a small amount of the milk to form a paste. Heat the rest of the milk in saucepan over medium heat. Add coriander, parsley, garlic and pepper. When milk mixture has heated but not boiled add cornflour, stirring continuously until it reaches a creamy consistency. Set aside.

Heat oil in frying pan over medium heat. Add onions and mushrooms. Cook until onions are transparent. Add cabbage, brussel sprouts, carrots, celery, garlic, soy sauce, spices and crumbled vegetable stock cube. Cook for 4 minutes.

Mix in the tinned mock meat, tomatoes, tomato sauce and crushed stock cube and cook for a further 3 minutes.

Place a 4cm (2in) thick layer of filling in a square cooking tin followed by one sheet of lasagne. Repeat twice more, finishing with a lasagne sheet. Pour sauce liberally over the top and cook in a moderate oven, 180°C (350°F) Gas Mark 4 for 45–50 minutes.

1 tablespoon cornflour

1 cup soy milk

½ teaspoon fresh coriander (cilantro), chopped

1 teaspoon fresh parsley, chopped

1 clove garlic, chopped

Pepper to taste

2 tablespoons oil

2 onions, diced

7 mushrooms, diced

¼ cabbage, shredded

4 brussels sprouts, diced

1 carrot, diced

1 celery, diced

3 cloves garlic, crushed

2 teaspoons soy sauce

2 teaspoons ground coriander

1 teaspoon black pepper

1 teaspoon dried basil

1 vegetable stock cube

1 teaspoon salt

440g can of any mock meat, diced

5 tomatoes, diced

½ cup tomato sauce

1 vegetable stock cube, crushed

4 lasagne sheets

Mains

Summer Lasagne

Serves 6

Place lasagne noodles in a shallow baking dish. Cover with hot water and sit 20–25 minutes. Drain.

Combine tofu, garlic, lemon juice, oil, and salt and pepper. Mix until smooth. Stir in the olives and capers.

Preheat oven to moderate 180°C (350°F) Gas Mark 4. Place walnuts on a baking sheet and lightly toast until fragrant. Remove from oven and place in a strainer, then rub skins off. Roughly chop.

Arrange a layer of lasagne sheets, cut to fit, on the bottom of a deep 23cm x 18cm (7in x 9in) glass baking dish. Place ratatouille on top, then spread ½ of the tofu mix evenly over vegetables. Top with another layer of lasagne, then vegetables, another layer of lasagne, finishing up with the remainder of the veggies. Spread the rest of tofu mix over evenly and sprinkle walnuts over the top.

Bake for 30 minutes or until juices bubble up around the sides of dish. Remove and let sit for a couple of minutes before serving.

12 lasagne sheets
500g (1lb) firm tofu
2 garlic cloves, peeled
2 tablespoon lemon juice
¼ cup extra virgin olive oil
½ teaspoon salt
Freshly ground black pepper
½ cup black olives, chopped
1 tablespoon capers, drained
½ cup walnut halves
Ratatouille (see recipe page 57)

Easy Pasta

Serves 4

Steam broccoli and tomatoes until soft. Place in saucepan and add mushrooms, garlic and tomato paste and stir. When hot and ready to serve, add pine nuts. Place on top of cooked pasta.

Enjoy with garlic bread.

1–2 heads broccoli
4 tomatoes, chopped
250g (8oz) mushrooms
Garlic, crushed—as much or as little as you like
1 small jar tomato paste
2 tablespoons pine nuts
375g packet of pasta, cooked

Our task must be to free ourselves by widening our circle of compassion to embrace all living creatures, and the whole of nature and its beauty.

Albert Einstein

Rainbow Spinach, Mushroom and Tofu Lasagne

Serves 6

Heat oil and fry the onions until light and golden. Add the garlic, oregano, basil, salt and pepper and cook for 1 minute. Add the tomato paste and tomatoes and bring to the boil. Simmer for a few minutes. Set aside.
To prepare the spinach, cut the stalk off cross-wise where it joins the leaf. Steam the spinach and mushrooms in a little water until tender. Allow to cool and chop roughly. Add any remaining liquid to the tomato sauce.

1 tablespoon olive oil
2 medium onions, finely chopped
2 cloves garlic, crushed
1 teaspoon dried oregano
1 teaspoon dried basil
½ teaspoon sea salt
Pinch ground black pepper
2 tablespoons tomato paste
400g crushed tomatoes
150g (5oz) firm tofu
½ bunch spinach
250g (8oz) mushrooms, sliced
1 packet spinach or wholemeal lasagne sheets—
sufficient to completely cover dish, overlapping a little
as you go (pre-soaking the sheets first makes them
easier to use)

Béchamel Sauce

1 ½ teaspoons wholewheat flour
1 cup water
1 cup soy milk
1 tablespoon ginger juice from freshly grated ginger
1 tablespoon tamari
2 teaspoon kuzu (wild Japanese arrowroot)
½ cup cold water

In a saucepan, mix flour and water and heat gently, stirring well. Add half the soy milk, the ginger juice and tamari. Bring to the boil. Add the rest of the soy milk. Mix the kuzu in cold water separately and then pour into the mixture, stirring well, until it thickens into a smooth sauce.

Another Soy Milk Topping Sauce

750ml (25fl oz) soy milk
¼ onion, sliced thinly
2 bay leaves
Pinch of sea salt
Pinch of cayenne pepper
60g (2oz) wholemeal or unbleached white flour
60g (2oz) vegan margarine

Place the soy milk, onion, bay leaves, salt and cayenne in a saucepan and bring to the boil. Lower to a very gentle heat and simmer for 5 minutes or until it thickens up and the consistency is creamy.

To Assemble

Preheat the oven to moderate, 180°C (350°F) Gas Mark 4.

Dip each sheet of lasagne into boiling hot water first to soften it up if you haven't presoaked, then lay the first sheets in the bottom of a greased tray, add a layer of vegetables, a layer of tofu and then the sauce. Make alternate layers of pasta, vegetables and sauce. As an extra spicy bonus I sometimes use a salsa tomato sauce as well as a white sauce. The salsa sauce has to be thick like a paste. To finish, I top the lasagne with wholemeal breadcrumbs and spot with vegan margarine so it won't burn the top.

Bake in the oven for 30 minutes or until golden brown. Let stand for 5 minutes and then serve with a crisp salad.

Curried Chickpea Burgers

(Gluten free)

Serves 4

Heat oil and sauté the onion until lightly browned, add the curry powder and cook until fragrant. Drain the chickpeas and lightly mash with a potato masher. Grate the carrots and zucchinis, squeezing out the juice (keep the juice aside, you may need it later). Add the vegetables to the chickpeas. Toss through the onion and curry powder mix, salt and pepper and enough flour to ensure the burgers will hold together. Add some of the carrot/zucchini juice if more moisture is needed.

Form into balls, roll in the remaining flour and the sesame seeds and place covered on a plate in the fridge to chill—this helps the burgers hold their shape.

Heat the remaining oil in a frying pan and place a couple of the burgers in the pan. Flatten with a spatula and flip to cook both sides. The burgers don't need to be cooked for very long, they just need to be brown on both sides.

Serve on a bun with avocado, tomato, lettuce and sweet chilli sauce.

1 tablespoon olive oil
1 brown onion, finely chopped
Indian curry powder, to taste
2 cups cooked or tinned chickpeas
3 medium carrots
2 zucchinis (courgettes)
Salt and pepper, to taste
¼ cup buckwheat flour (add more if needed for firm consistency)
2 tablespoons sesame seeds

The Meat Hater's Pizza

These days every pizza store seems to have some variation of a meat-lover's pizza—topped with four or five different types of dead factory-farmed animal. Beat the big corporate pizza chains at their own game with this yummy cruelty-free version.

Preheat oven to moderate, 180°C (350°F) Gas Mark 4.

Combine the dry ingredients for the dough in a large mixing bowl, then add the olive oil and water. Stir until your dough balls up and won't absorb any more flour. Now it's time to knead your dough: First sprinkle a little flour onto a clean benchtop and rub your hands with some flour to stop the dough sticking, then start kneading it. After a few minutes of kneading, your dough should be nicely combined and stretchy. At this point you can stretch it evenly across your pizza tray. This amount should make plenty of dough for a 12–14 inch (30–40cm) pizza tray, or several smaller trays.

To make the sauce: Sauté the garlic and onion in olive oil 2 minutes, then add the herbs, salt and pepper. Stir in your tomatoes and tomato paste and cook for another 5 minutes. This will make enough sauce for several pizzas. If it ends up too chunky for your liking, pop it into a blender for a few minutes.

Dough
2 cups plain flour
I packet (2¼ teaspoons) active dry yeast
I tablespoon sugar
I teaspoon salt
2 tablespoons olive oil
I cup warm water

Sauce
2 tablespoons olive oil
½ onion, finely chopped
2 cloves garlic, minced
½ teaspoon dried oregano
½ teaspoon dried basil
Salt and pepper, to taste
2 small-medium tomatoes, diced
¼ cup tomato paste

(Alternatively, if you're feeling lazy you can buy a pre-made pizza base and pizza sauce from the supermarket—watch out for milk solids and animal derived additives in the ingredients.)

Spread some pizza sauce over the dough, then add a liberal amount of barbeque sauce over the top. Grate some soy cheese over the sauces, then start adding your faux meats and tofu. Add some thinly sliced mushrooms and tomato, and possibly some fresh herbs, before grating more soy cheese over the top.

Pop your pizza into the oven and cook for 10–12 minutes, until the edges of the pizza base start to brown.

Toppings

Barbecue sauce

Meltable soy cheese

3 or more types of meat substitute, such as
   Veggie sausage, thinly sliced
   Veggie beef (e.g. burger patties cut into small chunks)
   Veggie mince (made from textured protein, onion, garlic, soy sauce and tomato paste)

Tempeh slices

Marinated tofu, cubed

Mushrooms, thinly sliced

1 fresh tomato, thinly sliced

Fresh herbs

Autumn Pasta

This recipe is somewhat unusual because it uses miso, a traditional Japanese ingredient, most often consumed as a soup.

Serves 6

Cook the pasta, drain and set aside. Heat the oil in a pan over a low heat, then fry the onion and garlic until they become translucent. Add the mushrooms and cook for about 1–2 minutes. Add the soy milk and coconut cream and simmer gently. Stir in the cashew paste, sesame oil, balsamic vinegar and miso until ingredients are well blended. Add the basil and desired amount of chilli and stir well. Toss through pasta and serve.

Make the sauce thinner by adding a little salted water, or thicker by adding a little plain flour as needed.

375g packet of penne or pasta of your choice
1 tablespoon extra virgin olive oil
1 small onion, chopped
1 large clove garlic, chopped
1 cup of dried shitake mushrooms or you can use any fresh mushrooms
1 cup soy milk
1 cup coconut cream
1 tablespoon cashew nut paste
1 dessertspoon sesame oil
1 dessertspoon balsamic vinegar
1 dessertspoon of miso paste
1 handful of basil leaves (or fresh herb of your choice), torn
1 teaspoon red chilli sambal or red chilli paste or half a fresh red chilli

Options
Sprinkle on sesame seeds and chopped cashews or fresh herbs and dried onions.
Use cooked aborio rice instead of pasta.

Greek Pasta Casserole

Cook the pasta in boiling salted water for 10 minutes or until tender. Drain, add 3 tablespoons of the butter and stir through, until melted. Set aside.

Place the savoury lentils, casserole mince, canned tomatoes and red kidney beans in a frying pan with onion, stock cube and salt and pepper. Cook while stirring over low heat for 10 minutes. Set aside.

Melt the remaining butter in a saucepan, add the flour and stir until doughy. Turn off the heat and add the soy milk gradually—stir until incorporated. Turn the heat back on and stir until the sauce has boiled and thickens slightly. Add salt, pepper and marjoram to taste and remove from heat.

Grease an ovenproof casserole dish of approximately 25cm by 25cm (10in x 10in). Lay half the pasta in the bottom of the dish, sprinkle over half the soy cheese, then spoon over the mince mixture. Layer the remaining pasta over the mince mixture, then spoon over the sauce mixture and spread evenly. Sprinkle the remaining soy cheese over the top.

Bake uncovered in a moderate oven, 180°C (350°F Gas Mark 4 for 30 minutes and serve with salad.

250g (8oz) vegan elbow or spiral pasta
½ cup soy butter or vegan margarine
¾ x 400g can savoury lentils
¾ x 415g can vegan casserole mince
400g can diced tomatoes
125g can red kidney beans
1 onion, peeled and finely chopped
1 vegetable stock cube, crumbled
Salt and pepper, to taste
¾ cup plain flour
2½ cups (600ml/20fl oz) soy milk
Fresh or dried marjoram, to taste
60g (2oz) grated soy cheddar or soy parmesan

Tempeh Slivers with Steamed Rice, Vegetables and Gado Gado Sauce

Heat oil, fry the onion, garlic and ginger gently for 5 minutes. Add the rest of the sauce ingredients. Cook at low heat for 10 minutes, adding water if the sauce gets thick.

Meanwhile, steam carrots, zucchini, broccoli, cabbage and celery together for 5 minutes.

Allow to cool, mix in the bean shoots.

Heat oil in a solid frypan, add the tempeh pieces. Cook until golden brown on each side, sprinkling lightly with soy sauce during cooking.

Place the rice on a plate or in a bowl. Top with the vegetables and pour the sauce over. Arrange the tempeh pieces on top and serve immediately.

Gado Gado Sauce

I tablespoon olive oil
I onion, finely chopped
I clove garlic, crushed
2 teaspoons grated ginger
I teaspoon chilli powder
250g (8oz) peanut butter
½ cup water
I tin coconut cream
I tablespoon vinegar or lemon juice
I tablespoon tamari or other soy sauce

I carrot, julienned
I zucchini (courgette), julienned
I head of broccoli, cut into florets
¼ cabbage, finely shredded
2 sticks of celery, julienned
2 handfuls fresh bean shoots
I tablespoons olive oil
300g packet tempeh, sliced thinly
I tablespoon tamari or other soy sauce
2 cups steamed brown rice

Sweet Potato Flan

Serves 6

Heat oil in a saucepan, then stir-fry onion, garlic, cardamom, ginger and chilli for 2 minutes. Add sweet potato and coconut cream and cook over a medium heat, covered, until sweet potato is very tender—20 minutes or so. Blend sweet potato mixture with tofu, then stir through coriander and pepper. Set mixture aside to cool. Spread mixture out in a prepared pastry shell (see recipe below) and bake in a moderate oven, 190°C (375°F) Gas Mark 4 for 30 minutes.

2 teaspoons oil, preferably sesame
I onion, finely diced
2 garlic cloves, crushed
I teaspoon ground cardamom
I teaspoon minced ginger
I teaspoon minced chilli
Ikg (2lbs) sweet potato, peeled and diced
¼ cup coconut cream
225g (7oz) tofu
¼ cup chopped coriander
Freshly ground black pepper
I prepared pastry shell
Additional chopped coriander for topping

Basic Wholewheat Pastry Makes 1 pastry shell

I cup (125g/4oz) wholemeal flour
¼ teaspoon baking powder
15g (½oz) melted vegan margarine
½ tablespoon oil
¼ cup water—the amount of water used is critical—add slowly
Additional flour

Sift flour and baking powder into a bowl and make a 'well' in the centre. Add margarine, oil and slowly add water, mixing as you go, gradually working the mixture by hand into a soft dough. Use extra flour to dust work surface, turn dough out and knead lightly for 30–60 seconds only. Roll out, place in to flan case and cut to size. Pastry shell is prebaked to prevent pastry going soggy.

Lentil Loaf

Soak lentils for 6 hours, cook for 20 minutes and drain. Cool. Heat oil and sauté onion and garlic until soft then combine with all the other ingredients. If too moist, add more breadcrumbs. Pack into a greased loaf tin and bake for approximately 1 hour in a moderate oven, 180°C (350°F) Gas Mark 4. Cool and turn out.

Serve with salad and red onion marmalade (see recipe page XX).

2 cups brown lentils
1 tablespoon olive oil
1 onion, finely chopped and sautéed
2 cloves garlic, minced and sautéed
1 red capsicum (bell pepper), finely chopped
12 black olives, pitted and finely chopped
1 tablespoon tomato paste
2 teaspoons egg replacer, pre-mixed with
* 4 tablespoons water*
Fresh breadcrumbs—1 large slice equivalent
220g (7oz) vegan cheddar cheese, grated

Pan Fried Tofu

Serves 6

Heat oil in a pan, then add, soy sauce, garlic, ginger and chilli. Add tofu and stir-fry for a couple of minutes until evenly coated with flavours. Toss in sesame seeds and serve.

1 tablespoon oil
2 tablespoons soy sauce
1 tablespoon minced fresh ginger
2 cloves garlic, crushed
Fresh chilli, to taste
150–200g (5–6oz) firm tofu, thinly sliced
2 tablespoons sesame seeds, toasted

Butterfly Bolognaise

Boil carrots until tender. In a saucepan, heat oil and cook onion and garlic until onions are translucent. Add pasta sauce, casserole bits, tomatoes, olives, basil, capers and carrots. Heat through.

In the meantime, boil butterfly pasta until soft. Drain. Pour sauce over pasta and add vegan parmesan cheese.

Serve with crispy thick bread.

2 carrots, chopped
2 tablespoons olive oil
2 large onions, roughly chopped
3 cloves garlic, chopped
500g (1lb) bottle pasta sauce
415g can casserole bits
2 tomatoes, roughly chopped
2 heaped tablespoons black olives, chopped
10–12 basil leaves, chopped
1 tablespoon capers
1 packet butterfly pasta
Vegan parmesan cheese to taste—
my son and I just keep adding as it's so delicious

Lentil Spaghetti Bolognaise

Soak the lentils in cold water for 1 hour prior to cooking. Heat oil in pan over moderate heat, then add onion, garlic, parsley and sage and cook until onions are golden. Add tomatoes and simmer for 5 minutes. Add lentils and stock and simmer, uncovered, until all stock is absorbed and lentils are tender—approximately 20–25 minutes.

Serve over spaghetti with crusty bread and a green salad.

Freezes well and tastes even better the second time round.

1 cup of green or brown lentils
2 tablespoon olive oil
1 onion, finely chopped
2 cloves of garlic, finely chopped
¼ cup flat leaf parsley, chopped
½ teaspoon sage
400g (can of diced tomatoes
375ml (12fl oz) vegetable stock
500g packet spaghetti, cooked

Mum's Vegetable Croquettes

Serves 6

Boil potatoes until tender, then mash. Melt vegan margarine in frying pan, add garlic, onion and curry powder and cook until lightly browned. Add carrot and zucchini and continue to cook until soft. Remove from the heat to cool slightly. Add egg replacer mix, crumbs and parmazano, mix well.

Shape mixture into croquettes. Combine extra crumbs with parsley and roll the croquettes in the mixture until coated.

Heat oil in frying pan, fry croquettes on both sides until golden brown. Drain on absorbent paper. Croquettes can be prepared several hours ahead and stored in fridge.

Serve with salad.

4 large potatoes, peeled
30g (1oz) vegan margarine
2 cloves garlic, peeled and chopped finely
1 small onion, chopped
1 teaspoon curry powder
1 small carrot, grated
2 small zucchinis (courgette), grated
1 teaspoon egg replacer, pre-mixed with 2 tablespoons water
2 tablespoon packaged breadcrumbs
2 tablespoons parmazano—vegan Parmesan cheese substitute
¼ cup breadcrumbs, extra
1 tablespoon chopped parsley
¼ cup oil—sufficient to coat base of non-stick frying pan, add as needed as croquettes absorb

My respect and empathy towards animals includes sea dwellers from dolphins to fish to lobsters. So, of course, I wouldn't dream of eating them. Alexandra Paul

Sunday (or Any Day) Roast

For some reason roasts have a reputation for being daunting to make, when in fact they are simple, quick to prepare, taste wonderful and present well.

The potatoes will take longest to cook, place in non-stick roasting pan that has been covered lightly—use a small brush to cover sides and bottom. Use the brush to cover the potatoes with oil. Place in hot oven, 220°C (400°F) Gas Mark 5, and cook for approximately 20 minutes then add the oil-covered carrots, pumpkin and onions and cook for a further 10–15 minutes.

Boil up a packet of frozen peas to serve on the side and there you have it...the perfect Sunday roast.

Vegetable oil
Potatoes, peeled and quartered (or halved, depending on size)
Carrots, peeled and halved
Pumpkin, cut into chunks, skin on
Onions, whole or halved
Frozen peas

Mains

94

Stuffed Spuds

These are limited only by your imagination. For a main meal you may like to provide 2 potatoes per person, for a side dish just the one—depending on how much of a carbohydrate addict you are.

Wash and blot dry the potatoes then cover in oil and salt. Take sharp knife and make a deep cross in the top and cover in foil —place in baking tray with baking paper to catch leaks. Cook in fan forced oven for approximately 1 hour on high heat—check intermittently with sharp knife to ensure cooked all the way through.

Once it's cooked, carefully (it's hot!), scoop out the insides and place in a bowl— ensure you have left the casing intact in the foil—use a teaspoon for the scooping out.

Mash the potato in the bowl and add any filling you desire.

With a spoon, put the mixture back into the potato shell and push down tightly. Cover with cheese and bake for 10 minutes. S erve with green salad.

I large potato per person
Vegan bacon or 'pepperoni'
Chopped black olives
Sun-dried tomatoes, cut finely
I tablespoon corn relish
Cracked black pepper
Vegan Edam or mozzarella cheese

Paella

Paella, considered Spain's national dish, is made from rice and a variety of ingredients, usually seafood. This paella has been adapted for vegans.

Serves 6

Rice

3 cups long grain rice, cover with water
2 teaspoons veggie stock powder
2 teaspoons dried arame seaweed
Pinch saffron or 1 teaspoon turmeric
Pepper and salt, to taste
1 tablespoon olive oil
1 large brown onion, finely sliced
2 cloves garlic, crushed
1 green capsicum (bell pepper), chopped
2 carrots, diced
300g packet vegan smoked sausage, diced
1 cup vegan fish pieces (available from Asian supermarkets)
2 zucchinis (courgettes), diced
1 cup peas
4 tomatoes, diced

Cover rice with water and bring to the boil. Add stock powder, seaweed, spice and seasoning and cook until the rice is cooked and water is absorbed.

Heat oil and add onion, garlic and capsicum for 5 minutes until soft. Add carrot and cook for a further 5 minutes.

Stir in remaining ingredients and cook for 15 minutes or until the vegetables are tender. Fold the rice through the vegetables and serve in a large bowl.

Easy Spinach Pie

Grease baking dish. Place half the filo pastry in the bottom. Mix spinach with onions, lemon juice, fetta, salt and pepper. Place other half of filo pastry on top. Brush margarine over filo and score pastry into triangles.

Place in very slow oven, 120°C (250°F) Gas Mark 1 for approximately 35–45 minutes until golden brown.

Serve with vegetables or salad and enjoy.

Butter or oil
375g packet of filo pastry
1 bunch of spinach, chopped
3 onions, chopped
Juice of 4 or 5 lemons
180g jar of vegan fetta
½ cup vegan margarine, melted
Salt and pepper, to taste

Loyalty to a petrified opinion never yet broke a chain or freed a human soul. Mark Twain, author.

Spinach and Tofu Pie

Serves 6–8

You can use bought flaky pastry for the crust or make your own pastry: Rub together the flour, margarine and salt. Add just enough water to make a soft dough. Roll out and line a 30cm (12in) greased pie plate, prick the bottom of the pastry shell lightly with a fork. Bake blind at 180°C (350°F) Gas Mark 4. (To bake blind take a circle of baking paper, weighted down with pastry off-cuts, rice or beans, place in dish containing pastry, then remove paper and weights after 5 minutes. This cooks the bottom a little before the filling goes in.)

Heat oil in the pan and soften the spinach and sauté the garlic. Add the nutmeg, salt and pepper then set aside. In a food processor, blend the tofu, tamari, soymilk, mustard, and sauce and then combine with the spinach. Pour into the pastry case and scatter nuts and seeds on the top. Bake in a moderate oven, 180°C (350°F) Gas Mark 4 for 30 minutes.

Garnish with tomato slices and herbs.

Pastry
2 cups of wholemeal flour, plain or self-raising
2 tablespoons vegan margarine or olive oil
Pinch of salt
Iced water

Filling
1 tablespoon olive oil
2 bunches chopped spinach
1–2 cloves garlic
Good pinch of nutmeg
Salt and pepper, to taste
500g (1lb) herb or marinated tofu
2 teaspoons tamari
½ cup soy milk
1 teaspoon mustard
Dash of red pepper sauce
Pine nuts or sunflower seeds
2 medium tomatoes, sliced
Parsley or basil, for garnish

Lentil Cottage Pie (Gluten free)

In a medium saucepan, heat a little olive oil and sauté the onion until lightly browned. Then add the garlic and celery and cook until fragrant. Next, place the tomatoes and tomato paste in the pan and cook until heated through. Add carrot, spinach, lentils and cook until spinach is soft. If this is too runny, make a paste of 1 teaspoon cornflour with a little water and add to mixture to thicken. Season.

In a separate saucepan of water, boil potato and sweet potato until very tender. Drain and mash with a fork while adding veggie stock (as a low fat option) or vegan margarine until smooth. Add salt and pepper to taste.

Spoon lentil mixture into a casserole dish then spread potatoes on top. Sprinkle with paprika or chilli powder if desired. Bake in a moderate oven, 180°C (350°F) Gas Mark 4 until a little brown on top.

Serve with a green salad.

Olive oil
1 medium brown onion, chopped
1–2 cloves of crushed garlic
1–2 sticks celery and leaves, finely chopped
½ cup crushed tinned tomatoes
2–3 tablespoons tomato paste
1 cup carrots, chopped or grated
1 bunch English spinach
2 x 400g (13oz) tins of brown lentils, drained
Salt and pepper, to taste
4 medium potatoes, peeled and chopped
1 medium sweet potato (kumara), peeled and chopped
¼ cup vegetable stock, optional
Vegan margarine, optional
Chilli powder or paprika, optional

Mexican Style Stuffed Capsicums

Cut capsicums in half lengthways, remove seeds and white matter. Heat oil and sauté onion and garlic, remove and set aside. Lightly brown bulgur wheat in dry pan, constantly shaking and stirring. Add tomato paste, basil, cumin, chilli powder, carrot, celery, onion and garlic. Add 2 cups of water, bring to boil and simmer. Stir until water is absorbed to prevent sticking and until the mixture is firm but moist. Fill halved capsicums with mixture.

Mix together tofu, breadcrumbs and stock powder and sprinkle on top of each filled capsicum. Bake on a shallow tray in moderate oven, 180°C (350°F) Gas Mark 4 for 10–15 minutes until capsicums are slightly crunchy. Turn off heat and check every few minutes until capsicums are only just tender. Do not overcook.

This recipe, prepared with larger quantities, is excellent for party finger food. It can be prepared in advance, refrigerated and then served hot or cold, with each capsicum half cut into two or three fingers according to size. My guests love this dish and always come back for seconds.

3 large red capsicums (bell peppers)
2 tablespoons olive oil
1 medium to large onion, finely chopped or grated
1 garlic clove, crushed
1 cup bulgur wheat
¼ cup tomato paste
1 teaspoon dried basil
1 teaspoon ground cumin
½–1 teaspoon Mexican chilli powder
1–2 large carrots, grated
2 sticks celery, grated
2 cups water
100–125g (3–4oz) hard tofu, grated
2–3 teaspoons dry breadcrumbs
Pinch of stock powder

Mum's Curried Sausages

Melt margarine in a large saucepan, add onion, sprinkle over curry powder and sugar and cook until onion is soft and translucent. Add carrots and capsicum. Add veggie stock and tomato sauce. When vegetables are almost cooked, add sliced sausages and peas. Cook for 5 minutes. Serve with rice or mashed potatoes

1 tablespoon vegan margarine

2 large onions, thinly sliced

1 dessertspoon curry powder

1 teaspoon raw sugar

2 large or 4 small carrots, thinly sliced

1 capsicum (bell pepper), thinly sliced

1 vegetable stock cube soaked in ¾ cup boiling water

2 tablespoons tomato sauce

2 x 300g packets vegan sausages sliced into 5cm (2in) pieces

1 cup baby peas

Being vegan helped me realise I can say and do what I believe is right. That's powerful.

Alicia Silverstone

Scrambled Tofu

For this recipe there is a lot of chopping, but once it's done it's very quick and easy to cook

For the side salad, which can either be incorporated into the scrambled tofu or just served with the meal, slice up mushrooms and baby spinach and place in frying pan with 2 teaspoons of the vegan margarine. Stir and cook until soft. A sliced up tomato can also be added.

Grab the whole packet of tofu and roughly break it up into bite-sized pieces with your hands. This promotes the 'scrambled' look much more than chopping it into squares.

Warm your frying pan, then add some olive oil and throw in your tofu. Stir and add soy sauce. Throw in 2 tablespoons of mustard seeds and stir. Now, begin adding tablespoons of turmeric; this adds flavour and gives it the yellow 'scrambled' look. Stir until all tofu is a yellowish colour, add a teaspoon or so of vegan margarine to make sure no tofu burns.

Finely chop up ginger, garlic, leek, shallots and the onion. Roughly dice tomatoes. Add to tofu. Keep stirring and keep it on relatively high heat. Once the tofu is soft and soaking up the turmeric, soy sauce and vegan margarine, and once all vegetables look soft, remove from heat.

Put all your tofu onto a bed of rocket. This can either be worked into the tofu or stay on the edges of the plate. Place your mushrooms and spinach either on top of tofu or to the side. Garnish with sweet chilli, soy or tahini. The tofu also works wonders on toast which has been heavily spread with avocado, so go wild.

This would normally feed two people for breakfast or one very hungry person. It is an excellent protein boost to start the day.

5 mushrooms
I cup baby spinach
3–4 teaspoons vegan margarine
I packet hard tofu
Extra virgin olive oil
2 tablespoons soy sauce
2 tablespoons mustard seeds
¼ cup turmeric
Snall piece of ginger
2 cloves garlic
I leek
I bunch shallots
I red onion
3 tomatoes
2 cups rocket lettuce

Suggested condiments
Sweet soy sauce
Sweet chilli sauce
Tahini

Mushroom & Asparagus Risotto

Serves 4

Heat oil in a pan and cook onion, garlic and ginger. Add mushrooms to the pan and lightly cook. Stir though the rice until coated in oil. Add stock, 1 cup at a time until absorbed. As you add the last cup of stock add the asparagus and continue to cook until all the liquid is absorbed.

You can add 6 tablespoons of vegan margarine to make this creamier—3 when frying onions and 3 at the finish when stock is absorbed.

Serve sprinkled with cheese and pepper.

I tablespoon olive oil
I onion, chopped—or 4 spring onions
I garlic clove, chopped
I teaspoon of grated ginger
2 cups of mushrooms, cleaned and sliced
I ½ cups arborio rice
3 ½ cups veggie stock
I bunch of asparagus, washed and chopped
I cup vegan parmesan cheese
Black pepper, to taste

Many things made me become a vegetarian, among them the higher food yield as a solution to world hunger.

John Denver

Coconut Korma

Serves 4

Heat a tablespoon of the oil in a large deep frying pan. Fry onion, garlic, ginger and cardamom pods for 5 minutes. Add curry paste, tomato puree, tomatoes and lentils. Cook for further 10 minutes.

Heat the remaining oil in a separate pan and stir-fry tofu for 5 minutes. Add the vegetables and spices, season and cook for 10 minutes. Stir in the tomato and lentil mixture. Add stock, cover and simmer for 20 minutes or until lentils are almost cooked, stirring occasionally. Stir in the coconut milk and coriander, reserving a little for garnish. Cook uncovered for a further 10 minutes. Garnish with coriander and serve with rice.

60ml (2fl oz) oil
125g (4oz) onion, sliced
2 cloves garlic, chopped
2½cm (1in) piece ginger, peeled and grated
3 cardamom pods, split
1 tablespoon curry paste
1 tablespoon tomato puree
400g (13oz) can chopped tomatoes
75g (3oz) red lentils
350g (11oz) tofu, cubed
500g (1lb) seasonal vegetables, chopped
    into bite-sized pieces
1 teaspoon ground coriander
1 teaspoon ground cinnamon
1 teaspoon ground cumin
1 teaspoon ground turmeric
Salt and pepper, to taste
600ml (20fl oz) vegetable stock
150ml (5fl oz) coconut milk
2 tablespoons chopped fresh coriander
Rice, to serve

Eggplant in a Carriage

First, make the batter, in a bowl put the flour, spices, salt, onion and basil and mix in water. Let it stand for ½ an hour.

Slice eggplant into ½cm (¼in) slices. In another bowl, mix the soy cream cheese, basil leaves, pepper, salt and olive oil and spread a thin layer between two slices of eggplant and press together firmly. Use up all of the eggplant this way.

Heat the oil in a solid fry pan. Dip each eggplant sandwich into the batter. Drop into hot oil a few at a time and cook until they are light golden brown. Remove from oil with slotted spoon and drain on absorbent paper. Repeat with the remaining slices.

Serve with an olive and basil tomato sauce

Batter

2 cups of besan (chickpea flour)
1 teaspoon sweet paprika
1 teaspoon garam masala
¼ teaspoon salt
1 small onion, finely chopped
6 fresh basil leaves, finely chopped
2 cups water

1 eggplant (aubergine)
1 heaped teaspoon of soy cream cheese
6 fresh basil leaves, finely chopped
Pepper and salt, to taste
1 teaspoon light olive oil
Olive oil for deep frying

Become a vegan/vegetarian: your body will respect you for your wisdom and the animals will love you for your compassion. Casey em, American Top 40 radio personality

Jaipur Subji (vegetables)

Heat oil and fry chilli, ginger, garlic, onions, turmeric and coriander, then add the raw vegetable of your choice and stir-fry for a few minutes. Add a little water, and put on the lid and simmer until vegetables are cooked. Before serving, add one small tin of coconut cream or coconut milk.

Serve with basmati rice. To cook rice, rinse 2 cups raw rice until water runs clean. Cover with one inch of water. Put on lid and steam on very low heat, without stirring, for about 12 minutes or until water is absorbed and rice is cooked.

2 tablespoons olive oil
1–2 fresh red chilli, chopped
1 teaspoon finely chopped fresh ginger
1 dessertspoon finely chopped fresh garlic
2 onions, chopped
½ teaspoon turmeric powder
1 bunch fresh coriander (cilantro), chopped
Raw vegetables i.e. chunks of cauliflower, carrots, broccoli, potatoes
1 small tin of coconut milk or cream
500g packet basmati rice

Taco Beans

Heat oil and fry the onion and garlic until translucent. Add remaining ingredients (or whatever veggies you like—mushrooms are nice too). Allow to simmer gently until the beans start to go mushy, add a little water if you like the beans runny. You can give it a bit of a mash with a potato masher too.

Delicious with brown rice, or in a taco shell with nice crisp lettuce and sliced tomato.

1—2 tablespoons olive oil
1 large onion, sliced
3 cloves garlic, sliced
750g (1 ½lbs) can kidney beans
2 tablespoons tomato paste
1 teaspoon paprika
½ teaspoon cumin
1 carrot, diced
1 zucchini (courgette), diced
½ red capsicum (bell pepper), diced

It is man's sympathy with all creatures that first makes him truly a man.

Albert Schweitzer, philosopher and 1952 Nobel Peace Prize recipient.

Salads & Dressings

Roast Pumpkin and Couscous Salad

Serves 4

Cut pumpkin into small pieces, spray with oil and, sprinkle with ground black pepper and roast in a moderately hot oven, 200°C (400°F) Gas Mark 5 until a skewer slips easily into flesh.

In a large heatproof bowl add 1½ cups of boiling water to the couscous and let it be absorbed. Heat oil and cook the onion and chilli for approximately 1 minute. Add the cumin and cinnamon and cook for another minute, then add the macadamia nuts and dates. Stir the above through the couscous.

Arrange rocket leaves on a plate, sprinkle the pumpkin over, then the couscous and finally add natural soy yoghurt and serve.

I wish it sounded more complicated as it tastes so good but that is it—enjoy.

1kg (2lbs) pumpkin,
Oil spray
Ground black pepper
1½ cups couscous
Boiling water
1 tablespoon oil
Large red onion, chopped
Fresh red chilli, chopped
2 tablespoons ground cumin
¾ tablespoon ground cinnamon
¾ cup macadamia nuts, roughly chopped
¾ cup pitted dried dates, quartered
Rocket leaves
175g tub plain soy yoghurt

The world's environment can no longer handle beef.

Jeremy Rifkin, author of *Beyond Beef*

Colourful Sunset Salad

Use ingredients which are in season for the best results.

Toss all ingredients together lightly to create a visual and sensory delight.

3 medium carrots, grated
2 small beets, grated
I cup fresh shredded coconut
½ cup parsley, chopped
Juice of I large orange
I cup currants
I cup alfalfa sprouts
I cup fenugreek sprouts
I cup mung sprouts
½ cup lentil sprouts
½ cup celery, chopped finely
½ cup sweet peas
I fennel bulb
Garlic chives for garnish

He is a heavy eater of beef. Methinks it doth harm to his wit. Shakespeare, *Twelfth Night*

Avocado and Grapefruit Salad with Lime Vinaigrette

Serves 2

In a small bowl, whisk together the olive oil, vinegar, lime juice, lime zest, black pepper, salt and sugar. Set aside.

Wash and pat dry the salad greens and arrange them in a flat bowl. Peel the grapefruit and carefully cut each segment out with a grapefruit knife or a sharp vegetable knife. All skin and pips should be removed from the segments. Peel and slice the avocado.

Arrange the slices of grapefruit and avocado on top of the salad leaves, then pour the vinaigrette over the top and sprinkle with chopped spring onions.

Serve immediately.

80ml (2½fl oz) extra virgin olive oil
1 tablespoon balsamic vinegar
1 tablespoon fresh lime juice
Zest of 1 lime
Ground black pepper
Pinch salt (optional)
Pinch sugar (optional)
Several handfuls of mixed baby salad greens
1 grapefruit—sweet pink variety best
1 ripe avocado
3 spring onions, finely chopped

To become vegetarian is to step into the stream which leads to Nirvana. Buddha

Watercress Coleslaw with Toasted Seeds

Serves 8

Combine the watercress, cabbage, carrots, and green onions in a large bowl. Toss gently to combine.

Place the yoghurt, mayonnaise and salt and pepper to taste in a medium bowl. Whisk well to combine.

Pour the yoghurt dressing and lemon juice over the watercress mixture and toss gently to combine.

Toast the seeds in shoyu sauce. Allow to cool. Toss through the roasted sesame and sunflower seed mixture.

Spoon into serving bowls and serve.

1 bunch watercress
¼ small red cabbage, finely shredded
2 medium carrots, coarsely grated
6 green onions, diagonally sliced
½ cup thick soy yoghurt
¼ cup vegan mayonnaise
Salt and pepper, to taste
Juice of 1 lemon
¾ cup sesame and sunflower seed toasted sprinkle mix
1 tablespoon shoyu sauce

I am a vegan now, and it was a conscious decision. I really wanted to be healthy. Brandy

Tangy Sprout and Orange Salad

Serves 6

Blend together the citrus juice and sunflower oil briefly. Add to the rest of the salad ingredients and toss together gently. Garnish with alfalfa and orange slices and serve.

Juice of 2 oranges
Juice of 1 lemon
50ml (2fl oz) sunflower oil
160g (5½oz) snow pea sprouts
100g (3½oz) bean shoots
1 medium carrot, cut into matchstick sized strips
1 red capsicum (bell pepper), thinly sliced
60g (2oz) button mushrooms, thinly sliced
2 shallots (spring onions), finely chopped
Grated rind of 1–2 oranges
Pinch sea salt
Freshly milled black pepper

Garnish
2 oranges, halved and sliced
½ punnet alfalfa sprouts

It takes less water to produce a year's food for a pure vegetarian than to produce a month's food for a meat-eater. John Robbins, *Diet for a New America*

Tabouli

Mix diced tomatoes (including the juices), shallots and cracked wheat. Let it stand for at least 30 minutes to allow the cracked wheat to become soft. Mix parsley, mint and allspice.

Just before serving combine the tomato mixture and parsley mixture together and add the rest of the ingredients.

I recommend adding the lemon juice a little bit at a time. Depending on taste you might like it more or less bitter.

2 medium tomatoes, finely diced
6 shallots, finely diced
¼ cup cracked wheat
1 bunch parsley, chopped
½ bunch mint, chopped
1 tablespoon of ground allspice
¼ cup olive oil
½ cup lemon juice
Salt to taste (optional)

Broccoli and Beetroot Salad

Divide broccoli into small heads, combine with onion and small cubes of beetroot. Add mayonnaise and mix through until ingredients are coated.

Serve on its own or on platter surrounded by green salad.

Large head of broccoli
½ red onion
1 cup fresh cooked beetroot or small can baby beets
Vegan mayonnaise

Mediterranean Tomato Salad

Serves 4–6

Toss all the ingredients very gently together to prevent the tomatoes from bruising and serve immediately.

6 medium firm tomatoes, cut into wedges
2 tablespoons very finely chopped onion
2 tablespoons chopped basil
1½ dozen Greek black olives
¼ cup olive oil
1 tablespoon lemon juice
Pinch salt and pepper

Buckwheat and Corn Salad

Serves 4

Place the buckwheat kernels in a pot with the water and salt. Bring to the boil, cover with a lid and cook on low heat until the buckwheat is tender and all the water has evaporated—approximately 15 minutes. Remove the lid and allow to cool.

Drained the tinned corn thoroughly (if using steamed corn, cut the niblets off the cob).

Shake the dressing ingredients together vigorously in a glass jar and pour over the cooled buckwheat, corn and chopped vegetables.

1 cup roasted buckwheat kernels
2 cups cold water
Pinch sea salt
440g (14oz) tin corn niblets
½ red capsicum (bell pepper), finely chopped
1 eschalot, finely chopped
1 stick celery, finely chopped

Dressing
Juice of ½ a lemon
¼ cup cold pressed sunflower oil
1 teaspoon dark sesame oil
1 teaspoon finely chopped fresh coriander
Freshly ground black pepper
1 teaspoon shoyu

Diabetes is not necessarily a one-way street. Early studies suggest that persons with diabetes can improve and, in some cases, even cure themselves of the disease by switching to an unrefined vegan diet.

Andrew Nicholson, M.D., Physicians Committee for Responsible Medicine

Greek Salad

Marinate tofu in miso and oil for 30 minutes. Wash and towel dry lettuce leaves—rip leaves and put into bowl. Add tofu and remaining salad ingredients.

To make dressing: Mix ingredients in a bottle and shake well.

Pour over salad and serve immediately.

I cup hard tofu, cut into small cubes
2 teaspoons white miso
2 teaspoons oil
I small lettuce, cut into chunk pieces
I red onion, cut into thin slices
2 tomatoes, cut in to wedges
½ continental cucumber, halved lengthwise
  and sliced

Dressing
¼ cup olive oil
¼ cup balsamic vinegar
I clove garlic, crushed
2 tablespoons fresh chopped basil
Pepper and salt, to taste
I teaspoon Dijon mustard

Couscous Salad

Heat olive oil over medium heat in a pan with a tight fitting lid, cook onion for 5 minutes until soft. Reduce heat and add garlic, spices, tomato paste and couscous and stir. Season with salt and pepper. Pour in stock, stir with a fork, then add capsicum, currants, pistachios and lemon and stir with a fork to separate grains.

Serve warm or at room temperature.

¼ cup olive oil
1 brown onion, thinly sliced
2 cloves garlic, crushed
2 teaspoons paprika
2 teaspoons coriander
1 teaspoon caraway seeds
2 tablespoons tomato paste
2 cups couscous
Salt and pepper
1½ cups boiling veggie stock or water
5 pieces sun-dried capsicum (or tomato), chopped
¼ cup currants
¼ cup shelled pistachios
1 tablespoon finely grated lemon rind

If you don't eat meat, you are certainly kosher and I believe that is what we should tell our fellow rabbis.

Rabbi Shear Yashuv Cohen, Ashkenazi Chief Rabbi of Haifa, Israel

Couscous for Two

Serves 2

In a microwave dish, combine couscous, salt, cinnamon, cumin and olive oil. Using a fork, mix it all together. Pour hot water over couscous mix until it is just covered. Cover container and let stand for at least 15 minutes. When time is up gently fluff the couscous with a fork using a circular motion. Be patient because if you try to hurry this step it will not become fluffy. Let it cool.

Fry eggplant in vegetable oil and place on paper towels to soak up the excess oil. Preheat oven to moderate, 180°C (350°F) Gas Mark 4. Put the rest of the ingredients on a baking dish and bake until capsicum is tender. Allow to cool.

After the vegetables and couscous have cooled, mix them together. Just before serving, warm up in the microwave on high for 1–2 minutes and fluff it up again with a fork.

For a special touch you can sprinkle some fresh coriander and nuts over the top. I really enjoy it with toasted Lebanese bread brushed with olive oil mixed with a clove of crushed garlic.

1 cup couscous
½ teaspoon salt, optional
½ teaspoon ground cinnamon
½ teaspoon cumin
1 tablespoon olive oil
Boiling water

Vegetables
1 small eggplant (aubergine), diced
1 red capsicum (bell pepper), diced
1 red onion, diced
1 clove garlic, diced
½ teaspoon cinnamon
½ teaspoon cumin
½ teaspoon salt, optional
1½ tablespoons olive oil

Vegan Mayonnaise

This is a light, creamy mayonnaise, particularly suitable for livening up a tossed green salad.

In a pan, heat soy milk and arrowroot powder, stirring to thicken.

Meanwhile, place water and rolled oats into a blender or food processor. Blend well and slowly add enough oil to thicken—approximately ½ a cup. Add the cooled mixture. Blend, then add garlic powder, onion powder, paprika, mustard or celery salt, lemon juice, salt and pepper.

Pour into screw top jar and chill, preferably for a few hours, before using.

1 cup soy milk
1 ½ tablespoons arrowroot powder
1 cup water
1 ½ cups rolled oats
Oil
¼ teaspoon garlic powder
½ teaspoon onion powder
½ teaspoon paprika
1 teaspoon prepared mustard or ½ teaspoon celery salt
¼ cup lemon juice
Salt and pepper, to taste

Omega 3 Salad Dressing

This is a relatively low-fat salad dressing that is high in Omega-3s and other essential fatty acids. I use it not only on salads, but on all kinds of foods, including rice and vegetable dishes.

Combine all ingredients in a jar or bowl and stir well.

185g (6oz) freshly squeezed lemon juice
125g (4oz) flaxseed oil
125g (4oz) extra virgin olive oil
125g (4oz) soy sauce
1 large clove garlic
¼ onion
¼ cup hemp seed

Basic Vinaigrette

Makes about 1 cup

½ cup extra virgin olive oil
¼ cup balsamic or apple cider vinegar, to taste
1 tablespoon Dijon mustard
1 tablespoon honey, maple syrup or brown
  rice syrup
1 teaspoon Italian or all-purpose seasoning

Combine all ingredients in a bottle and shake thoroughly. Shake well before each use.

Walnut Vinaigrette

250ml (8fl oz) olive oil
250ml (8fl oz) walnut oil
150ml (5fl oz) white wine vinegar
Salt and pepper, to taste
Squeeze of lemon

Combine ingredients in a small bowl and whisk.

I am conscious that meat eating is not in accordance with the finer feelings, and I abstain from it whenever I can.

Albert Schweitzer, M.D., philosopher and Nobel Peace Prize recipient

Baking & Desserts

Sienna Cake

This is a famous Tuscan cake.

Sienna cake is very popular, will keep for a long time in your refrigerator and is served in small slices as it is rich.

Bake the nuts in a moderate oven, 180°C (350°F) Gas Mark 4 for just a few minutes until they are golden. When cool, chop roughly and place in a mixing bowl. Add in the glacé fruit, raisins, peel, flour, drinking chocolate and cinnamon.

Line a 20cm (8in) round cake tin with greaseproof paper.

Melt dark chocolate in a double boiler or in microwave.

Place the golden syrup and sugar in a saucepan with a small amount of water. Boil for 5 minutes until it bubbles and starts to caramelise. Add the melted chocolate and the liquid sugar to the fruit and flour mixture. Mix well together and spread evenly into the tin. Bake in slow to moderate oven, 160°C (325°F) Gas Mark 3 for 35 minutes. Let cool and do not cut until the next day.

Sift icing sugar thickly over the top before serving.

125g (4oz) blanched almonds
125g (4oz) hazelnuts
60g (2oz) glacé cherries
60g (2oz) glacé pineapple
60g (2oz) glacé apricot
60g (2oz) raisins
60g (2oz) mixed peel
¾ cup plain wholemeal flour
½ cup drinking chocolate
1 teaspoon cinnamon
½ cup granulated sugar
½ cup golden syrup
50g (2oz) 85% cocoa dark chocolate
Icing sugar—sifted as snow on top of finished cake

Glazed Sugar-free Orange Poppy Seed Cake

Mix the dry ingredients, then add the wet ingredients. Add extra orange juice if needed to make the mixture not too runny but not too dry either. Pour in a to a greased 20cm (8") cake tin. Bake in a moderate oven, 180°C (350°F) Gas Mark 4 for 50–60 minutes.

Bring glaze ingredients to the boil in a pan over a low heat and let simmer for 1minute then pour over the cake when cool.

1½ cups spelt flour
1 cup buckwheat flour
cup poppyseeds
2 teaspoons baking powder
1 tablespoon vegan margarine, melted
1 cup orange juice
Grated rind of 1 orange
¼ cup pear juice concentrate

Glaze
¼ cup rice malt syrup
¼ cup orange juice
2 tablespoons orange rind

As custodians of the planet it is our responsibility to deal with all species with kindness, love and compassion. That these animals suffer through human cruelty is beyond understanding. Please help to stop this madness.

Richard Gere

Chocolate Orange Cake

Preheat oven to moderate, 190°C (375°F) Gas Mark 4.

Combine dry ingredients (sifting will help but is optional). In a separate bowl, mix together zest and all the liquids, except vinegar, and then add these to the dry ingredients. Mix until smooth, and then add vinegar. Pour into a greased 20 x 20cm (8 x 8in) baking tray and put into oven as soon as possible or all the gas from the vinegar/soda reaction will escape.

Bake for 25–30 minutes or until a fork or skewer comes out clean. Let it rest before slicing.

1 ½ cups flour
⅓ cup cocoa powder
1 teaspoon baking soda
1 cup sugar
½ cup vegetable oil
⅔ cup orange juice
⅓ cup soy milk
2 teaspoons vanilla essence
2 tablespoons vinegar
Zest of 1 orange

The Quintessential Carrot Cake

Mix all the dry ingredients together, making sure there are no lumps of soda or baking powder. Add oil, pineapple and carrot and mix well.

Pour into a greased and lined 20cm (8in) x 10cm (4in) loaf tin or round tin. You can also make 12 large muffins, 6 monster muffins or 24 small muffins.

Bake in a moderate oven, 180°C (350°F) Gas Mark 4 for 35 to 40 minutes.

Icing

In a small bowl, beat the vegan margarine until soft. Beat in the icing sugar and vanilla. When the cake is cool, swirl the icing mixture over the top of the cake and serve.

1 cup plain wholemeal flour
1 teaspoon baking powder
¾ teaspoon bicarbonate of soda
¼ teaspoon ground cloves
½ teaspoon ground ginger
½ teaspoon cinnamon
½ cup chopped walnuts
½ cup sugar
½ cup olive oil
440g (13oz) tin crushed pineapple
1 cup grated carrot

Icing

500g (1lb) vegan margarine
250g (8oz) icing sugar
½ teaspoon vanilla essence

Fur used to turn heads, now it turns stomachs.
Rue McClanahan

Wholemeal Shortbread Biscuits

Mix the flours and sugar together. Rub in the margarine with your fingertips until a coarse breadcrumb texture is achieved. Add the vanilla essence and quickly roll the dough into a ball. Do not over-work. On a lightly floured surface, roll the dough into a rectangle 1cm (½in) thick. Cut into fingers and bake in a preheated moderate oven, 180°C (350°F) Gas Mark 4 for 5 minutes. Turn over and cook for a further 2–10 minutes until golden brown on both sides. Cool on a wire rack.

125g (4oz) wholemeal flour
125g (4oz) unbleached white flour
60g (2oz) raw sugar
200g (6½oz) vegan margarine
10 drops vanilla essence

Note
For variety you can add rolled oats, desiccated coconut or chopped ground almonds or hazelnuts in place of a similar weight of flour. eg 150g (5oz) wholemeal flour and 100g (3oz) desiccated coconut equals 250g (8oz).

Mango and Blueberry Pie

Serves 8

Place the dates in a bowl. Juice and grate the rind of lemon and pour over the dates. Allow to soak.

Grind almonds finely in a food processor, remove to a bowl.

Blend dates separately in food processor until they form a paste. Add ½ the date paste to the ground almonds and mix thoroughly. Press into a 23cm (9in) tart shell which needs no cooking.

Then prepare the filling. Puree the blueberries and add the remaining date paste, vanilla and cinnamon. Set aside.

Peel the mangoes and slice. Arrange half on the piecrust. Then pour the blueberry puree on top. Top with the remaining mango slices. Garnish with flaked almonds and blueberries. Place in fridge and chill.

Pastry Crust
200g (6½oz) dates (half used for the filling)
I lemon
250g (8oz) almonds

Filling
250g (8oz) blueberries
I teaspoon vanilla
¼ teaspoon cinnamon
3 large mangoes
Flaked almonds, toasted and blueberries for garnish

Vegan Vanilla Slice

Line the base and the sides of a 23cm (9in) square deep tray with foil. Place pastry sheets onto a lightly greased oven tray and bake in hot oven, 220°C (450°F) Gas Mark 6, for 6 minutes or until golden brown. Allow to cool. Then gently flatten pastry with your hand and fit one of the sheets into the base of the foil-lined tray, brown side up.

Mix sugar, cornflour and custard powder in a pan. Gradually stir in soy milk until smooth and well combined. Add margarine and stir over heat until mixture boils and thickens.

Reduce heat and stir for another 2–3 minutes. Remove from heat and add the rum and vanilla essence. Mix thoroughly.

Pour hot custard over the pastry in the tray. Place second pastry sheet over custard with the browned side down. Press down slightly. Allow to cool. Place passionfruit icing over the pastry. If necessary, smooth the icing surface by dipping a knife into hot water and then running it over the icing surface. Refrigerate.

Cut into slices when cooled and set.

2 sheets ready rolled puff pastry
1 cup caster sugar
½ cup cornflour
½ cup custard powder
1 litre (1¾ pints) soy milk
60g (2oz) vegan margarine
2 teaspoons rum essence
2 teaspoons vanilla essence

Passionfruit Icing
2 cups icing sugar
60g vegan margarine
2 tablespoons passionfruit pulp

Passionfruit icing
Place sifted icing sugar into a small heatproof bowl. Add margarine and passionfruit pulp. Stir through until smooth. If needed, add extra pulp to make a smooth paste that is easy to spread.

Chocolate Cake

Mix together the vegan margarine, dates, pear juice concentrate, soy milk and vinegar. Sift in the dry ingredients and stir to combine.

Pour into a greased and lined 20cm (8in) x 10cm (4in) loaf tin or round tin.

Bake at 180°C (350°F) Gas Mark 4 for 30–40 minutes. When cool, ice and top with strawberries or nuts.

Bring icing ingredients to the boil slowly. Simmer for 1 minute. Take off the heat.

¼ *vegan margarine*
½ *cup dates, finely chopped*
3 *tablespoons pear juice concentrate*
4 *tablespoons soy milk (add as much as needed)*
1 *teaspoon vinegar*
1½ *cups spelt flour*
1 *cup buckwheat flour*
¼ *cup soy flour*
2 *teaspoons baking powder*
½ *teaspoon bicarbonate of soda*
¼ *cup cocoa*

Icing
¼ *cup vegan margarine*
¼ *cup cocoa*
4 *tablespoons soy milk*
¼ *cup pear juice concentrate*

Pumpkin Muffins

Makes 6 large or 12 small muffins

Preheat oven to moderately hot, 200°C (400°F) Gas Mark 5 and grease muffin tins.

Blend margarine and sugar into bowl. Beat egg replacers and fold into the pumpkin puree with soy milk. Fold the flour into the wet mixture and place in muffin tins. Sprinkle with cinnamon sugar and bake for approximately 20–25 minutes.

¼ cup vegan margarine
½ cup sugar
Egg replacer for 2 eggs
1–1½ cups pumpkin puree
½ cup soy milk
1½ cups self-raising flour

Tofu Pumpkin Bars

Preheat oven to 180°C (350°F) Gas Mark 4. Blend the tofu and banana. Add apple sauce, pumpkin and sugar. Add the flour, baking powder and spices and mix to combine. Bake for 25 minutes.

Allow to set for 5 hours before cutting into bars.

120g (4oz) soft tofu
½ mashed banana
1 cup apple sauce
2 cups pumpkin
1 cup sugar
2 cups plain flour
1 tablespoon baking powder
1 tablespoon cinnamon
1 teaspoon ground ginger
1 teaspoon ground nutmeg
1 teaspoon ground allspice

Banana Sunflower Seed Cake

(Sugar free)

Mix together the bananas, soy milk, pear juice concentrate and vegan margarine. Add the seeds and the sifted flours and baking powder. Mix well until light and fluffy. Pour into a greased and lined 20cm (8in) x 10cm (4in) loaf tin or round tin. Bake in a moderate oven at 180°C (350°F) Gas Mark 4. for 50–60 minutes.

3 ripe bananas, mashed
½ cup soy milk (add more if it is too dry)
¼ cup pear juice concentrate
½ cup melted vegan margarine
½ cup sunflower seeds
I cup spelt flour
I ½ cups buckwheat flour
3 teaspoons baking powder

Apple Apricot Loaf

Cream the margarine. Add the pear juice concentrate, soy milk and orange juice then add other ingredients. Pour into a greased and lined 20cm (8in) x 10cm (4in) loaf tin or round tin. Bake in a moderate oven, 180°C (350°F) Gas Mark 4 for 50–60 minutes.

½ cup vegan margarine
¼ cup pear juice concentrate
½ cup soy milk
¼ cup orange juice
I cup spelt flour
I cup buckwheat flour
2 teaspoons baking powder
I ½ teaspoons cinnamon
½ teaspoon nutmeg
2 apples, finely chopped
½ cup dried apricots, chopped

Aussie Cockie Seed Cake

Mix dry ingredients all together in a large bowl. Then combine the coconut milk and maple syrup and mix in with other ingredients. Place the mixture in a greased and lined tin and bake for 1 hour in a moderately slow oven, 160°C (325°F) Gas Mark 3. It is cooked when a skewer through the centre comes out clean.

Remove from oven and leave in the tin for 5 minutes before turning out onto a cake rack to cool.

1 cup sunflower seeds
2 cups mixed dried fruit
1 cup macadamia nuts
1 cup sugar
½ cup shredded coconut
2 cups self-raising flour, sifted
2 cups coconut milk
¼ cup maple syrup

Banana Blueberry Cake (Sugar free)

In a bowl, sift flours and baking powder. Add the wet ingredients and mix. Pour into a greased and lined 20cm (8in) x 10cm (4in) loaf tin or round tin. Bake in a moderate oven, 180°C (350°F) Gas Mark 4 for 50–60 minutes.

1 cup spelt flour
1½ cups buckwheat flour
2 teaspoons baking powder
½ cup fresh or tinned blueberries
3 ripe bananas
¼ cup pear juice concentrate
½ cup melted vegan margarine
½ cup soy milk

Berry and Apple Crumble

Grease a 20cm (8in) baking dish. Place the sliced apples on the bottom and top with berries.

With your fingers rub together the flour, vegan margarine, brown sugar and cinnamon until finely crumbed, then spread evenly on top of the berries.

Bake in a preheated moderate oven, 180°C (350°F) Gas Mark 4 for 40 minutes.

4 large apples, peeled and thinly sliced
500g (1lb) mixed berries, fresh or frozen
½ cup vegan margarine
1 cup dark brown sugar
1 cup wholemeal self-raising flour
1 tablespoon cinnamon

Compassion is the foundation of everything positive, everything good. If you carry the power of compassion to the marketplace and the dinner table, you can make your life really count. Rue McClanahan

Baked Bananas

Serves 4

Cut bananas in half and place in greased casserole dish. Cover with juice, brown sugar and rind and dot with knobs of vegan margarine and sprinkle with rum. Cover with foil and cook at 180°C (350°F) Gas Mark 4 for 15 minutes. Remove from oven, serve with vanilla soy ice cream and sprinkle of Curacao (Laraha liqueur).

4 bananas
Juice of an orange
Brown sugar
Rind of an orange
1 tablespoon rum, optional
Vegan margarine

Fig and Apple Loaf

Remove any stems from the figs, core the apple and roughly chop. Cover with brandy. Roast nuts in a moderate oven, 180°C (350°F) Gas Mark 4 for 5–7 minutes. Leave to cool.

Sift flours, salt, baking powder and cinnamon together then return sifted bran from the wholewheat flour to the mix. Add sugar then stir in oil, banana and soymilk. Fold in the fruit and nuts and scrape into a greased and lined 10 x 23cm (4 x 9in) loaf tin. Bake in a moderate oven, 180°C (350°F) Gas Mark 4 for 1–1¼ hours or until a skewer comes out clean. Cool completely before cutting.

120g (4oz) dried figs
175g (5½oz) green apple
1 teaspoon brandy
150g (5oz) walnuts
75g (2½oz) flour
75g (2½oz) wholewheat flour
Pinch salt
2 teaspoons baking powder
2 teaspoons cinnamon
125g (4oz) brown sugar
80ml (2½fl oz) olive oil
1 mashed banana
2 tablespoons soy milk

Coconut Cake

Lightly grease a 20cm (8in) cake tin. Sprinkle sides with a ¼ cup of the coconut. In a large mixing bowl, beat the vegan margarine, coconut essence, sugar, egg replacer, and coconut cream until pale and thick. This will take about 5 minutes. Fold in the flour and remaining desiccated coconut.

Make up egg replacer equivalent to 2 egg whites in a small bowl or mug. Beat with a fork until frothy. Fold into mixture. Pour into cake tin. Bake in a moderate oven 180°C (350°F) Gas Mark 4 for about

1 cups desiccated coconut
250g (8oz) vegan margarine
1 teaspoon coconut essence
1 cup caster sugar
Egg replacer for three whole eggs and two egg whites
¾ cup coconut cream
1½ cups self-raising flour

45 minutes or until a skewer comes out of the cake relatively cleanly. This cake is especially nice with coconut frosting and fresh strawberries.

Pear Upside Down Pudding

To make the topping: Melt margarine, add brown sugar and stir until melted. Pour into 20cm (8in) cake tin and arrange pears on top, cut side up.

To make the pudding: Sift together flour, egg replacer, soda, salt & spices. In another bowl stir sugar, golden syrup, soy milk and melted margarine together until well mixed. Add flour mix to this and beat well. Pour over pears. Bake in a moderate oven, 180°C (350°F) Gas Mark 4 for 40–45 minutes. Cool slightly before turning out. Serve with soy ice cream or soy cream.

Topping
60g (2oz) margarine
100g (3½oz) brown sugar
6 canned pear halves

Pudding
125g (4oz) plain flour
2 teaspoons egg replacer
½ teaspoon bicarbonate of soda
Pinch of salt
1 teaspoon ground ginger
¼ teaspoon nutmeg
¼ teaspoon cinnamon
125g (4oz) brown sugar
90g (3oz) golden syrup
½ cup soy milk
60g (2oz) melted margarine

Human beings are the only animals of which I am thoroughly and cravenly afraid. George Bernard Shaw.

Tofu Cheesecake with Fruit Topping

Sift together both flours and rub in margarine with fingertips until the mixture resembles breadcrumbs. Wrap and chill for one hour or more. Using fingertips, press into an 18cm (7in) pie dish to make a crust of even thickness. Prick the bottom with a fork and bake in a hot oven at 230°C (475°F) Gas Mark 5 for 10 minutes.

Puree the tofu in 2 batches in a blender until smooth, then mix into a bowl with the remaining filling ingredients. Spoon filling into base and bake in moderate oven, 180°C (350°F) Gas Mark 4 for 30–35 minutes or until the filling has set, risen a little and is golden yellow on top. Allow to cool to room temperature.

To make the topping: Combine the strawberries, ½ a cup of the apple juice, the maple syrup and salt in a small saucepan and bring to the boil.

Dissolve cornflour in remaining juice, quickly stir into fruit mixture until thick and clear, then pour topping over cooled pie. Allow topping to cool and set and serve the cheesecake chilled.

Base
55g (2oz) wholemeal flour
115g (4oz) plain flour
115g (4oz) vegan margarine

Filling
455g (14½oz) tofu
2–4 tablespoons tahini
115ml (3½fl oz) pure maple syrup
2 tablespoons lemon juice
½ teaspoon sea salt
1½ teaspoons pure vanilla essence

Strawberry Topping
115g (4oz) strawberries, whole
¾ cup apple juice
¼ cup pure maple syrup
Pinch salt
1½ tablespoons cornflour

Date and Walnut Rolls

To make the syrup: Boil syrup ingredients together in saucepan, reduce until bubbles are a light amber.

Combine dates, walnuts, golden syrup, orange peel and cardamom in a food processor and blend until a paste forms.

Preheat oven to moderately hot, 200°C (400°F) Gas Mark 5. Remove 1 sheet filo and place on work surface, brush with oil. Top with second sheet, brush with oil. Add another sheet if you really like filo pastry. Place date mixture across the top and roll. Brush the surface with oil and roll in sesame seeds. Repeat this process until all pastry and filling are used. Bake until golden, about 23 minutes. Trickle a little of the sugar syrup over hot date rolls. Retain remaining syrup and pour over with vegan yoghurt when serving.

Serve with soy yoghurt.

Sugar Syrup
I cup water
I cup sugar
I cinnamon stick
Lemon juice

250g (8oz) pitted dates
½ cup walnuts
¼ cup golden syrup
I teaspoon finely grated orange peel
½ teaspoon ground cardamom
375g packet filo pastry
I cup light oil
½ cup sesame seeds

Black Forest Cherry Cake

Drain the tinned cherries and soak them in the liqueur the night before you make this cake.

On the day, preheat the oven to moderate, 180°C (350°F) Gas Mark 4, and grease a 20cm (8in) round cake tin.

Drain the cherries, reserving the liqueur and cherries separately. Beat the margarine and sugar until creamy. Add the egg replacer and vanilla essence then fold in the flour and cocoa. Mix in the bicarbonate of soda, coffee, coffee liqueur and milk, then blend until smooth. Pour into the cake tin and bake for about 30–40 minutes.

To make chocolate cream: Melt the chocolate and margarine and beat until very creamy. Set aside to cool.

Once cake is cooked, remove from the tin and allow to cool on a tray. Once completely cooled, slice through the middle. Spread lightly with some of the mock chocolate cream and pour over the reserved cherries, spreading them evenly. Place the top back on the cake and cover in the remaining chocolate cream. For decoration you can melt some chocolate and pour onto greaseproof paper and harden in the freezer. Once hard, break into shards and place around the edge of the cake.

425g (13½oz) tin of pitted cherries
1 cup coffee liqueur (for example Tia Maria)
200g (6½oz) vegan margarine
1 cup caster sugar
3 teaspoons egg replacer
1 teaspoon vanilla essence
1½ cups self-raising flour
½ cup of cocoa
1 teaspoon bicarbonate of soda
1 tablespoon instant coffee
2 tablespoons soy milk

Mock Chocolate Cream
200g (7oz) dark chocolate
250g (8oz) vegan margarine

Jelly Tart

Crush the biscuits in a food processor then add the vegan margarine and mix. Grease a flan tray and press the mix into the tray. Refrigerate until the base is set.

Peel and slice the kiwi fruit and arrange on top of the base then slice the other fruit and arrange. Make up the jelly according to the directions and pour over the fruit—covering all the fruit and coming up to the top of the sides of the base. Place in the fridge to set and serve cool.

1 packet of plain biscuits
375g tub vegan margarine
2 kiwi fruit
1 banana
1 punnet of strawberries
1 peach or pear
85gm packet of vegan jelly

The closer you can live to being a vegetarian the better.

Gary Player

Butterscotch Schnapps Cheesecake

Crush the biscuits in a food processor then add to the vegan margarine and mix. Grease a 26 x 26cm (10 x 10in) flan tray and press the mix into a tray. Refrigerate until the base is firm.

With a hand mixer, blend the pudding mixes, soymilk and cream cheese until you get a fairly firm consistency then blend in the schnapps. You may need to use more soy milk (or schnapps if you are not driving) just to get it to the consistency you'd like. (Do not worry about the directions on the pudding pack.)

Pour into base and put back into the fridge for at least 1 hour.

I like to decorate this by melting dark chocolate and placing in a piping bag and making circles around the top of the tart, starting from the outer and moving into the middle with smaller circles. Then get a skewer and from the centre, make lines all the way around so that it looks like a cobweb.

375g packet vegan shortbread or ginger biscuits
¾ cup vegan margarine
2 x 80gm packets vanilla pudding mix
1 cup soy milk
227g tub vegan cream cheese
¼ cup butterscotch schnapps
Dark chocolate for decorating (optional)

Dawn's Lemon Pie

Make crust by combining cookie crumbs, brown sugar and margarine. Press in to flat 20cm (8in) ovenproof dish and bake in moderately slow oven, 160°C (325°F) Gas Mark 3, for 10 minutes. Allow to cool.

Whisk sugar, soy milk, orange juice, cornstarch and salt together in a medium saucepan with a heavy bottom. Stir over medium heat until thick then let boil for 1 minute. Remove from heat and whisk in lemon juice, zest and margarine.

Pour lemon filling into crust and chill.

1 cup cookie crumbs
¼ cup brown sugar
¼ cup vegan margarine
1 cup white sugar
½ cup soy milk
½ cup orange juice
½ cup cornstarch
¼ teaspoon salt
½ cup lemon juice
2 tablespoons lemon zest (or 2 teaspoons lemon extract)
1 tablespoon vegan margarine

I became a vegetarian out of concern for animals, but I wasn't a vegetarian long before I realised there's something to that. I don't think I would have worked for the past five years were it not for my vegetarian diet. Bob Barker

Maryland's Mum's Pineapple Upside-down Cake

Spread brown sugar evenly in 23cm (9in) cake tin (Maryland uses a cast iron frying pan with handle) and arrange pineapple pieces on sugar mixture. Set aside.

To make the cake batter: Beat together sugar, egg replacer and olive oil. Add lemon juice or soy milk, vanilla essence and beat well. Stir in flour until well combined.

Pour cake batter carefully over sugar mixture in tin. Bake in moderate oven at 170C for about 50 minutes but check before that.

Cook cake in pan for 5 minutes then invert on serving plate or tray and let stand 1 minute before serving. Best when served warm but just as delicious when cold.

1 cup firmly packed brown sugar
6 slices pineapple, drained and sliced in half

Cake batter
1 cup sugar
Egg replacer for 2 eggs
3 tablespoons olive oil
½ cup lemon juice (or soy milk)
1 teaspoon vanilla (optional)
Then add 1 cup sifted self-raising flour

Mango Rice Pudding

Cook rice, mango juice, cinnamon sugar, coconut milk, maple syrup and water on low heat for approximately 15 minutes. Stir constantly so mixture doesn't stick. Take off heat, keep covered but stir every so often until liquid is absorbed. Check rice is soft. Add slices of mango.

Gently re-heat if necessary, before serving with vanilla soy ice-cream.

1 cup arborio rice
2 x 425g cans sliced mangoes, drain and reserve juice
1 dessertspoon cinnamon sugar
1 cup coconut milk
1 tablespoon maple syrup
½ cup water

I don't understand why asking people to eat a well-balanced vegetarian diet is considered drastic, while it is medically conservative to cut people open and put them on cholesterol-lowering drugs for the rest of their lives.

Dean Ornish M.D.

Gingered Figs

Wash figs. Place in a saucepan and cover with water. Add 1 tablespoon of the lemon juice, 2 tablespoons of the lemon peel and ginger. Simmer until soft. Remove figs from liquid and place in a serving dish. Reduce liquid until syrupy—add more sugar and lemon juice to taste. Pour syrup over the figs and chill.

Great with baked apples or bananas.

250g (8oz) dried figs
Juice and sliced peel of 2 lemons
Large piece of root ginger
¼ cup palm sugar

Other things being equal, I judge that a strict vegetarian will live ten years longer than a habitual meat eater, while suffering on the average, less than half so much from sickness.

Horace Greeley (1811–1872), American newspaper editor
and founder of the *New York Herald Tribune*

Fig and Walnut Sourdough

Levain or sourdough starter culture is simply created by mixing wholegrain or wholemeal flour (preferably organic) with water and leaving. It is refreshed with more flour and water after bubbles appear (about 3 days), and every day thereafter. Within a week you should have a live culture. You are basically encouraging the wild yeast (saccharomyces exiguous) and lactobacillus bacteria, normally occurring in the grains, to grow and create the fermentation process.

The refreshment ("feeding") ratio of water to flour is 1:1 and it is best to start with about 100–150g (3–5oz) of flour.

The sourdough starter culture creates its own antibiotic which is why it does not go off, unless contaminated with something else.

For more information on sourdough starter see www.wildsourdough.com.au.

Makes 3 free-form loaves of bread

Place all ingredients in a mixing bowl, mix vigorously for 3 minutes with a wooden spoon or spatula.

Rest the dough for 15–20 minutes to let the flour swell and absorb the water.

Take your dough to a cool flat surface. You may need to adjust the water and flour at this stage as you knead the dough—it needs to be soft and slightly sticky. Knead for a full 10–15 minutes.

The dough should feel elastic and soft, and have a silky sheen.

150g (5oz) biodynamic/organic rye starter culture, ripe and at room temperature

650g (1¼lbs) biodynamic/organic 50% premium bakers flour or unbleached white spelt

150g (5oz) biodynamic/organic wholegrain rye flour

250g (8oz) biodynamic/organic unfiltered apple juice, at room temperature

250g (8oz) filtered water, at room temperature

15g (½oz) sea-salt, finely ground

300g (9½oz) biodynamic/organic dried figs, cut into quarters

150g (5oz) biodynamic/organic sultanas

150g (5oz) biodynamic/organic walnuts, chopped roughly

Let the dough rest at room temperature to rise for 5–12 hours until doubled in bulk—usually the rising time is about 5–8 hours.

Divide the dough into 3 pieces. Carefully form a rectangular shape with each piece of dough, and then scatter the dried fruits and nuts evenly.

Roll tightly and shape the dough into three elongated 'batons'.

Rest the loaves for a final 2 hours at room temperature then carefully score the dough with a sharp serrated knife.

Preheat oven to hot, 225°C (450°F) Gas Mark 6 and bake loaves for 10 minutes, then reduce the oven to 210°C (425°F) gas Mark 5 for a further 20–25 minutes. Turn oven off, and let the loaves sit in the oven for a further 30 minutes.

Leave to cool in the tins for 15 minutes before turning out onto wire rack to cool completely.

The greatness of a nation and its moral progress can be judged by the way its animals are treated.

Mahatma Gandhi

Banana, Sunflower and Pistachio Bread

Preheat oven to moderate, 180°C (350°F) Gas Mark 4. Grease and line base of 23cm (9in) loaf tin.

Beat the vegan margarine or prune puree and sugar until light and creamy. Add egg replacer gradually, beating well. Stir in bananas, nuts and seeds.

Sift together flour, bicarbonate of soda and mixed spice, then fold into banana mixture.

Spoon into the tin and bake for 1 hour or until skewer comes out clean when inserted into centre.

Leave to cool in the tin for 15 minutes before turning out onto wire rack to cool completely.

Serve with vegan margarine.

100g (3oz) vegan margarine
¾ cup brown sugar
Egg replacer for 2 eggs
500g (1lb) ripe bananas mashed
100g (3oz) shelled pistachio nuts, roughly chopped
½ cup sunflower seeds
2 cups self raising wholemeal flour
1 teaspoon bicarbonate of soda
¼ cup mixed spice

Beer Bread

Mix together ingredients, put in greased 20cm x 12cm bread tin and bake for 40 minutes at 190°C (375°F) Gas Mark 4.

This is a really quick, yummy, moist bread. Good with a winter soup.

3 cups self-raising flour
1 dessertspoon sugar
1 teaspoon salt
440ml (14fl oz) beer

Note

Some beer and wine are clarified to remove impurities and for aesthetic reasons—this can be done using egg whites, whole milk, casein, gelatine or Isinglass (made from the bladders of sturgeon fish). Please be aware that many beers and wine are not vegan friendly.

The Gods created certain kinds of beings to replenish our bodies, they are the trees and the plants and the seeds. Plato

Condiments & Drinks

Mum's Zucchini Pickles

Wash vegetables and slice. Combine in a glass or pottery bowl with salt and sufficient water to cover. Leave overnight.

Drain and rinse.

Combine sugar, vinegar and spices in a pan over heat and stir to dissolve sugar. Bring to boil, add vegetables. Boil again and then lower heat and simmer for 5 minutes. Put into sterilised jars, allow to get cold, seal and store in fridge.

1kg (2lbs) zucchini (courgette), ends trimmed
1 red capsicum (bell pepper)
1 green capsicum
2 onions
1 stick celery
¼ cup salt
1½ cups white sugar
2 cups white vinegar
1 teaspoon mustard
1 teaspoon celery seeds

Prune Puree (Butter or margarine replacement)

Makes 1 cup

Blend all ingredients together in a blender or food processor until smooth. Puree can be refrigerated for 2 weeks.

1 cup pitted prunes
³⁄₈ cup water (just a little less than ¼ cup)
2 teaspoons vanilla essence
2 teaspoons corn syrup

Cashew Cream

Blend all ingredients until the mixture reaches a uniformly smooth consistency. The amount of milk may need to be increased depending on the strength of your blender or your own personal preference. This base can then be used to make smoothies (blend in your favourite fruits and extra milk), dessert creams (add chocolate powder or vanilla essence, and by replacing half the cashews with pecans you get an unexpected coffee flavour). Cashew cream can also be used as a thickener in other sweets.

2 cups cashews, raw and unsalted
2 large ripe bananas
1/3 cup soy/rice/grain milk

Easy Stir-fry Sauce

In a bowl mix equal quantities of the ingredients and add this to your favourite stir-fried veggies just before you take them out of the wok–it's as easy as that!

For something different, try adding some freshly grated ginger to the mix, or chopped Thai basil leaves, or spice it up with slices of hot chilli.

Tamari (wheat free soy sauce)
Sweet chilli sauce
Sesame oil

Note
Please check the ingredients of the sweet chilli sauce as not all brands are vegan friendly.

Parmesa-Almond (Substitute for Parmesan cheese)

Just mix and keep in a jar in refrigerator. Great to sprinkle on pastas and minestrone soup.

I cup of ground almonds
½ cup of nutritional yeast (vegan brand)
¼ cup of salt

Red Onion Marmalade

Heat olive oil and sauté onions until soft–add everything else and simmer until caramelised. This marmalade keeps for weeks in the fridge.

150ml (4fl oz) olive oil
4 red onions, finely sliced
3 teaspoons grated ginger
¼ cup brown sugar
100ml (3fl oz) white vinegar
50ml (1½fl oz) balsamic vinegar
100ml (3fl oz) marsala
½ teaspoon ground cloves
Touch of chilli

You ask people why they have deer heads on the wall. They always say 'because it's such a beautiful animal'. There you go. I think my mother is attractive, but I have photographs of her. Ellen DeGeneres

Red or Green Curry Paste

1 ½ teaspoon coriander seeds

1 teaspoon cumin seeds

1 teaspoon fennel

1 teaspoon peppercorns

4 cloves

20 x chillies (red or green) seeds removed

¼ cup olive oil

2 large shallots (spring onions), peeled and sliced

1 bunch coriander (cilantro), chopped

1 stalk lemon grass, chopped finely

2 slices ginger

¼ grated nutmeg

zest of half a lime

Squeeze of lime juice

Pinch of salt

Blend all ingredients until smooth.
Refrigerate.

Orange Salsa

(right)

½ red onion, finely chopped

1 red capsicum (bell pepper), finely chopped

3 tomatoes, chopped

3 oranges, chopped

2 tablespoons olive oil

Salt and pepper

½ bunch mint, finely chopped

½ bunch parsley, finely chopped

Mix together.

Too Easy Soy Shake

I have one of these every second night whether I need it or not. They are so yummy, quick and delicious and yes, good for you.

Large glass of cold creamy soy milk
One large banana or blueberries, mangoes
**   strawberries; whatever is in season**
3 heaped tablespoons soy protein powder

In a blender (or with a hand held beater) blend until foaming.

Dad's Lemon Cordial

My son and I have carried our respective childhood addictions to Dad's cordial into adulthood. He always used homegrown lemons.

950ml (1¾ pints) water, boiled
1kg (2lbs) white sugar
1 tablespoon citric acid
1 cup lemon juice

Combine ingredients, stirring until sugar is dissolved. Allow to cool, pour into sterilised bottles and keep refrigerated.

Animals are my friends and I don't eat my friends.

George Bernard Shaw

Conversion Guide

Measures

1 level teaspoon–5g (¼oz)

1 level tablespoon–20g (⅔oz)

1 heaped tablespoon–30g (1oz)

1 liquid pint – 600ml (20fl oz)

1 litre–1000mls (1¾ pints)

1 teaspoon liquid–20ml (⅔fl oz)

1 cup–250ml (8fl oz)

Liquids

1 cup–250ml (8fl oz)

4 cups–1 litre (1¾ pints)

Volume

20ml (⅔fl oz)–1 tablespoon

30ml (1fl oz)–½ tablespoons

40ml–2 tablespoons

50ml–2½ tablespoons

60ml (2fl oz)–3 tablespoons

65ml–¼ cup

100ml (3fl oz)–5 tablespoons

125ml (4fl oz)–½ cup

250ml (8fl oz)–1 cup

1.25 litres (28fl oz)–5 cups

Cup Measures

1 cup flour–140g (4½oz)

1 cup rice syrup–375g (12oz)

1 cup fresh breadcrumbs–60g (2oz)

1 cup rice, uncooked–220g (7oz)

1 cup mixed fruit or individual fruit
    eg sultana–185g (6oz)

1 cup nuts, chopped–125g (4oz)

1 cup coconut desiccated–90g (3oz)

Contributors

I would like to give my heartfelt thanks to the many enlightened family members and friends who contributed their tried and true vegan recipes to this book—I couldn't have done it without you.

SOUPS

Chunky Mexican Bean Soup	Kristi-Anna Brydon
Quick and Yummy Soup	Christine Townend
Carrot and Cumin Soup	Claudette Vaughan
Russian Borscht	Claudette Vaughan
Savoury Lentil Soup	Claudette Vaughan
Corn and Split Pea Chowder	Lynette McQueen
Riz-U-Marsh	Claudette Vaughan
Thai Pumpkin Soup	Claudette Vaughan
Italian Pumpkin and Bean Soup	Margaret Setter
Parsnip Soup	Linda Williams

ENTREES

Vietnamese Rice Paper Rolls	Bach-Tuyet & John Mancy
Beetroot Tapenade	Animal Liberation
Olive Tapenade	Animal Liberation
Coriander and Peanut Pesto	Animal Liberation
Broad Bean Puree with Rocket	Animal Liberation
Aubergine Paté	Animal Liberation
Nasudengaku (*Eggplant Grilled with Special Miso Paste*)	
From Shu Sugisaki of the wonderful Sapporo Japanese Restaurant	
Char-Grilled Capsicum & Sunflower Dip	Animal Liberation
Baba Ghanoush	Animal Liberation

SIDE DISHES

Rosemary and Garlic Potatoes	Claudette Vaughan
Mema Lorrie's Tsimmis	Scott Krauss and Anthony Fletcher

MAINS

Huevos Rancheros	Derryn Hinch
Easy Mushroom Pie	Kristi-Anna Brydon
Seitan in Red Wine With Rosemary	Kylie Dubrich
Quick and Easy Vol au Vents	Mark Pearson
Mushroom Risotto	Angie Stephenson
Lentil Bobotie	Diana Mitchell
Greek Stuffed Eggplant	Diana Mitchell
Red Lentil Dahl	Claudette Vaughan
Tofu Kofta Bake	Claudette Vaughan
Gourmet Vegan Quiche	Margaret & Kylie Dubrich
Creamed Vegetables with Gnocchi	Jon Hackett
Spinach Stew	Jon Hackett
Vegetable Lasagne	Jon Hackett
Easy Pasta	Susanne Briggs
Rainbow Spinach, Mushroom and Tofu Lasagne	
	Claudette Vaughan
Curried Chickpea Burgers	Kristi-Anna Brydon
The Meat Hater's Pizza	Drew Fryer
Autumn Pasta	Danielle Archer
Greek Pasta Casserole	Lana Went
Tempeh Slivers with Steamed Rice, Vegetables and Gado	
Gado Sauce	Diana Mitchell
Sweet Potato Flan	Christina Sumner and Dave Best
Lentil Loaf	Christina Sumner and Dave Best
Paella	Diana Mitchell
Easy Spinach Pie	Susanne Briggs
Spinach and Tofu Pie	Brenda Glasgow
Lentil Cottage Pie	Kristi-Anna Brydon
Mexican Style Stuffed Capsicums	Margaret Setter
Scrambled Tofu	Jacqueline Dalziell
Mushroom & Asparagus Risotto	Linda Williams

186

Never Fail Vegan Pizza | Claudette Vaughan
Coconut Korma | Andrea Simpson

SALADS

Roast Pumpkin and Couscous Salad | Linda Williams
Couscous for two | Denise McKay
Tabouli | Denise McKay
Couscous Salad | Joanna Sumner
Greek Salad | Diana Mitchell
Broccoli and Beetroot Salad | Fiona Eyre
Mediterranean Tomato Salad | Claudette Vaughan
Buckwheat and Corn Salad | Claudette Vaughan
Italian Green Salad | Diana Mitchell
Watercress Coleslaw with Toasted Seeds | Claudette Vaughan
Tangy Sprout and Orange Salad | Claudette Vaughan
Colourful Sunset Salad | Claudette Vaughan
Avocado and Grapefruit Salad *with Lime Vinaigrette* | Kate Summer
Vegan Mayonnaise | Margaret Setter
Walnut Vinaigrette | Claudette Vaughan
Omega 3 Salad Dressing | John Robbins

CONDIMENTS & DRINKS

Cashew Cream | Jonathan Hallett
Easy Stir-fry Sauce | Kristi-Anna Brydon
Parmesa-Almond | Diana Mitchell
Red Onion Marmalade | Christina Sumner and Dave Best
Orange Salsa | Claudette Vaughan
Red or Green Curry Paste | Claudette Vaughan

BAKING

Fig and Walnut Sourdough | Yoke Madewi-Caddy
Beer Bread | Joanna Sumner
Banana, Sunflower and Pistachio Bread | Tammy Atkinson
Chocolate Cake | Amanda Quinn
Chocolate Brownies | Matt Wade
Vegan Vanilla Slice | Jonathan Hallett

Black Forest Cherry Cake | Margaret Dubrich/Kylie Dubrich
Pear Upside Down Pudding | Jessica Bailey
Chocolate Orange Cake | Harrison Swift
Orange Poppy Seed Cake *with Glaze for Cake* | Amanda Quinn
Banana Sunflower Seed Cake | Amanda Quinn
Apple Apricot Loaf | Amanda Quinn
Banana Blueberry Cake | Amanda Quinn
Strawberry Shortcake | Georgina Topp
The Quintessential Carrot Cake | Diana Mitchell
Berry and Apple Crumble | Maria Armstrong
Tofu Pumpkin Bars | Claudette Vaughan
Aussie Cockie Seed Cake | Colleen Russell
Mango and Blueberry Pie | Claudette Vaughan
Wholemeal Shortbread Biscuits | Claudette Vaughan
Tofu Cheesecake with Fruit Topping | Claudette Vaughan
Sienna Cake | Diana Mitchell
Fig and Apple Loaf | Claudette Vaughan
Coconut Cake | Michele Warner
Baked Chocolate Custard | Tammy Atkinson
Date and Walnut Filo Rolls | Diana Mitchell
Pumpkin Muffins | Tammy Atkinson
Baked Cheesecake | Bede Carmody
Easy Vegan Chocolate Cake | Drew Fryer
Dawn's Lemon Pie | Nona, Louis and Xanthe

DESSERTS

Jelly Tart | Kylie Dubrich
Butterscotch Schnapps Cheesecake | Kylie Dubrich
Chocolate Mousse | Amanda Quinn
Gingered Figs | Claudette Vaughan
Maryland's Mum's Pineapple Upside-down Cake | Maryland Wilson

Additional Reading

The China Study, Professor T. Colin Campbell, 2005;

'White Lies', Vegetarian and Vegan Foundation 2006;

Devil in the Milk: Illness, Health and Politics. A1 and A2 milk, Professor Keith Woodford, 2007;

'Nurses Health Study', Harvard University, *American Journal of Clinical Nutrition*, University of California 2000

Index